How To Use Water Power

by Herbert Chatley

with an introduction by Roger Chambers

Self Reliance Books

Get more historic titles on animal and stock breeding, gardening and old fashioned skills by visiting us at:

http://selfreliancebooks.blogspot.com/

Introduction

I am pleased to present yet another title on Homesteading and Farm Life.

This volume is entitled "How To Use Water Power" and was published in 1907.

The work is in the Public Domain and is re-printed here in accordance with Federal Laws.

As with all reprinted books of this age that are intended to perfectly reproduce the original edition, considerable pains and effort had to be undertaken to correct fading and sometimes outright damage to existing proofs of this title. At times, this task is quite monumental, requiring an almost total "rebuilding" of some pages from digital proofs of multiple copies. Despite this, imperfections still sometimes exist in the final proof and may detract from the visual appearance of the text.

I hope you enjoy reading this book as much as I enjoyed making it available to readers again.

Roger Chambers

Fig. 11—C. E. COLBURN'S FARM AND STOCK BARN

1

Fig. 19—Mr. Lawson Valentine's Barn, "Houghton Farm," Mountainville, N. Y.

2

PREFACE.

THIS little book has been designed to meet what I believe is a felt want. The subjects referred to are of increasing importance ; but the study of it is almost prohibited to those who cannot spare the time to study applied mechanics in the lump.

There are many excellent works on the subject in English, French, and German, but the majority are too mathematical for the young engineer to tackle at first.

I have endeavoured to produce not an exhaustive treatise, but a clear account of the methods and principles of Hydraulic Engineering as at present practised, in a form that can be easily grasped by the craftsman or student with limited knowledge of mechanics and mathematics. There are many things which could be more thoroughly treated, but I have thought it better to sacrifice further discussion to my main purpose, viz., simplicity and utility.

I must confess my indebtedness in many respects to the following works, to which I refer the inquirer for further information : Blaine's "Hydraulics," Prof. Perry's "Applied Mechanics," Prof. Cotterill's "Applied Mechanics," Weisbach's "Geschichte des Maschinen," etc.

I would call especial attention to the chapters on Tidal Power, Sewage, and Water Supply, chiefly derived from experience.

CONTENTS.

ILLUSTRATIONS.

———

*(Photos. from Fielding and Platt, Gloucester; Tangyes, Birmingham;
and Gilbert Gilkes, Kendal.)*

HOW TO USE WATER POWER.

CHAPTER I.

SOURCES OF POWER.

THE use of water for the supply of power to machinery is an extremely important branch of modern engineering practice.

From it has resulted immense improvement in the handling of materials and artillery, the testing of materials, the use of lifts, swing bridges, mill machinery, and electricity generation.

We must commence a study of the manner in which water power is used by considering under what conditions water naturally exists.

We have usually nearest to hand an underground store of more or less pure water due to the accumulation of rain and spring water upon impervious layers of soil.

In order to use this we must raise it (by pumping), so that in its descent again the energy which pumping gave it is to some extent recovered.

Next we have rivers and streams containing large volumes of water in motion, which motion may be available for power supply.

Further, there are springs at high levels which enable us to store up large quantities at a fairly great height above the ordinary level at which work is to be done.

Fourthly, we have the sea, which by its tides can alone supply immense power, and also is a source of water for pumping.

A little consideration of these states will show us that *still* water can only do work in virtue of its *height*. This is termed potential energy.

Moving water may have power to do work on account of remaining height (potential energy again); it may have velocity (kinetic energy) on account of the height from which it has descended, and it may have pressure, due to local changes in the velocity resulting from alterations of the channel, etc. Now, a very strict investigation into natural phenomena has shown us that energy is indestructible, so that if *still* water possesses a certain amount of potential energy (*i.e.*, height), when it is allowed to move this must re-appear in some one of the three forms mentioned (— loss by friction), so that if we consider the energy which 1 lb. of water possesses we can balance the conditions of its changes while moving as follows :—

STILL	=	MOVING	
Total head	=	Velocity head	+ Pressure head
(*i.e*, height above lowest level it can descend to).		(*i e.,* the height which corresponds to its particular speed).	(*i.e.,* the height which corresponds to its particular pressure).
		+ Remaining potential head	+ Friction head
		(*i.e.,* the height yet to be descended).	(the height which corresponds to the energy lost as heat by rubbing against sides of channel).

We thus have a means of comparing the work-producing ability of still and moving water. It cannot be too clearly understood that in both cases the energy is derived from intrinsic height (technically termed "head"), and that if such "head" does not exist in water for hydraulic power it must be imparted by some other source of power, usually a pump worked by heat engine or electric motor.

The total amount of work which can be done by water is found by multiplying the weight in pounds by the total *available* head in feet. The result, which being the product of feet and pounds is called "foot-pounds," is when divided by the time during which it can be used (minutes) the *power* (*i.e.*, rate of doing work). It is customary to regard 33,000 foot-pounds per minute (= 550 foot-pounds per second) as the unit of power, so that the following expression gives us the work possible from water :—

$$\frac{\text{weight in lbs.} \times \text{available head (net) in feet}}{\text{time in minutes} \times 33000}$$
$$= \text{H.P. which water can supply.}$$

Now as to what this "available head" is. If we store up spring or rain water in a *reservoir* or tank so that a certain constant level is maintained above that at which we wish to have power, this difference of height is the available head. If the tank level falls during use, then we must take the net height at any one time.

If we pump water into a tank or into a "hydraulic accumulator" (described later), we give it altogether a "head" which is measured by the total height to which the water is raised (or for an accumulator the *equivalent* height to which water would be raised if the load is considered as water—see later), but as part of the height is between the ground and the surface of the supply water (this part height being called the "suction head") we must deduct so much from the total imparted head to get the head available for power purposes.

Hence available head = total imparted head − suction head. Seeing that all the energy we use is in the first place supplied by some engine to the pumps, we only use hydraulic power in connection with pumping when its advantages over other power systems are peculiarly applicable to the work to be done, as is the case with pressing machinery, hoists, lifts, and artillery.

In the case of running water we must determine three things :—

(1) How much *below* the permanent level of the water at the works we can put our machinery. This is the measure of the potential head or available height. Say "h_1" feet (potential head).

(2) What velocity the water is running with. This is obtained by observing the motion of floats, or by the measurement of the quantity passing in a certain time with "gauges." This velocity in feet per second squared, divided by 64, is a measure of the equivalent height (the fall from which would produce such a velocity), and can be taken as a further part of the available head. Say

$$\frac{(\text{velocity})^2}{64} \text{ (feet per second)} = h_2 \text{ feet (velocity or kinetic head)}.$$

(3) When there are changes in the channel the velocity will not be constant, and in order to compensate for this variation in energy we find certain pressures appear (we must carefully distinguish between these and that which occurs when the motion of the water is purposely opposed).

To put this into other words, where the motion of the water is resisted some of the velocity-energy changes to pressure, causing a tendency to rise in the water, which will make small tributary channels have higher levels than the general stream. If such an extra height is observed at any particular place (as against a dam or weir) this in feet is called the pressure head. If it is possible to find the pressure in pounds per square inch, this multiplied by 2·3 will give the equivalent head of water thus :—

Observed pressure head or 2·3 × pounds per square inch pressure = h_3 (pressure head).

Now by the conditions of balance previously referred to the velocity and pressure heads are the equivalent of the head behind (less friction against the sides of the channel) which is driving the stream, so that at the works we realise the total head of the stream above our working level in three forms—velocity, pressure, and remaining height (not to the mouth of the river, but only to our working level).

Next as to the style of machinery we employ.

Potential head is of itself not capable of being used, but changed into pressure and velocity it can be employed, and we therefore have two classes of machinery, which we can call (A) presses (using pressure) (B) water motors (using pressure and velocity).

Before considering these in detail we must remind the reader as to the convertibility of the three states :—

h_1	h_2	h_3
Potential.	Pressure.	Velocity.
Height in feet.	$\dfrac{\text{Height in feet}}{2\cdot 3}$ = lbs. per sq. in.	Square root of $(64 \times \text{height})$ = velocity ft. per sec.

These are in each case considered for each 1 lb. of water, and remembering that one gallon = 10 lbs. and 1 cubic foot of water = 62½ lbs., we have the following rules for cases where N gallons of water are available with potential pressure or velocity-energy :—

Potential.	Pressure.	Velocity.
$10 \times N \times \text{height}$ = work that can be done by water possessing actual head.	$10 \times N \times$ pressure in lbs. per sq. in. $\times 2\cdot 3$ = work available from pressure of water.	$\dfrac{10 \times N \times (\text{velocity})^2}{64}$ = $\dfrac{N \times (\text{velocity})^2}{6\cdot 4}$ = work that can be done by water possessing a velocity of so many feet per second.
Can only be used by conversion into pressure or velocity.		
Can be stored only as potential.	Can be changed into potential or velocity with loss.	Can be changed into pressure or potential with loss.
The original source of power.	Used in hydraulic press with slow motion.	Used in water motors (wheels, turbines, hydraulic ram, etc.).

We can now see that three things must be considered in arranging for hydraulic power :—

(1) The quantity of water available.

(2) The form of its energy, *i.e.*, potential, pressure or velocity.

(3) The equivalent total head.

To simplify the general description of machinery we will make a little table showing the way in which each affects the problem. (Details of each are explained later.)

	Title.	Quantity (Weight).	Energy.	Head supplied (Perfect conditions).
SOURCES OF POWER.	Reservoir of water at high level naturally.	Contents of reservoir $\dfrac{\text{in gallons} \times 10 = \text{lbs.}}{\text{cubic ft} \times 62\frac{1}{2} = \text{lbs.}}$	Entirely potential; can be used as pressure, or, by letting it flow freely, as velocity.	Height above working level.
	Stream or waterfall.	Velocity in ft. per sec. $\times$ cross area in sq. ft. $\times$ 62$\frac{1}{2}$ = lbs. per sec.	Chiefly velocity; pressure by resistance, and head by remaining full to working level.	$\dfrac{v^2}{64} + 2\cdot3\,p + h_3$ $(h_1) + (h_2) + (h_3)$
	Pump.	Capacity of pump in cub. ft $\times$ strokes per sec. $\times$ 62$\frac{1}{2}$ = lbs. per sec.	Chiefly pressure; energy stored as potential when used for reservoir.	Equivalent height above working level $(2\cdot3p)$ - suction head.
	Bramah press.	Capacity in cub. ft. $\times$ strokes per sec. $\times$ 62$\frac{1}{2}$ = lbs. per sec.	Pressure (velocity almost nil).	$2\cdot3\,p$.
MACHINES.	Water-wheel.	Capacity of bucket $\times$ number per sec. $\times$ 62$\frac{1}{2}$ = lbs. per sec.	Chiefly pressure (some velocity).	$2\cdot3\,p$ (p = resultant pressure, lbs. per sq. in.)
	Turbines.	Area of outlets in sq. ft. $\times$ radial velocity $\times$ 62$\frac{1}{2}$ = lbs. per sec.	Chiefly velocity; converted into pressure by impact.	About $\dfrac{v^2}{32}$ where v is velocity of rim.
	Rams.	Area of supply pipe $\times$ velocity ft. per sec. $\times$ 62$\frac{1}{2}$ = lbs. per sec.	Velocity and pressure.	$\dfrac{v^2}{64} + 2\cdot3\,p$.
	Hydraulic engine.	Cylinder capacity $\times$ strokes per sec. $\times$ 62$\frac{1}{2}$ = lbs. per sec.	Pressure.	$2\cdot3\,p$.

CHAPTER II.

TRANSMISSION AND LOSS OF POWER.

THE great advantage of water power lies in the facility with which it can be transmitted without great loss, being only excelled in this respect by electrical energy. There are, however, certain limitations to which it is subject, and we must, therefore, consider somewhat generally certain important properties of fluids which concern the transmission of power in it.

(1) Water is almost incompressible.
(2) It transmits pressure equally in all directions with very little internal friction unless there is at the same time rapid motion.
(3) It presses at right angles to every surface immersed in it, such pressure, if only the result of gravity, being proportional to the depth, and having a mean value at the centre of gravity of the immersed surface.

Next we have to consider what happens when it moves. Firstly, why and when does it move? Well, it moves when there is a difference of pressure in two parts, which would, when it is still, be balanced. This is the characteristic of all motion. Balance takes place by the appearance of a motion (or rather an acceleration, i.e., an alteration in velocity) in precisely that direction and magnitude which a balancing force would have.

In order to compare the result with the force of gravity (which is the only standard we have) we divide the weight of the water (or other body) concerned by 32, the result being called the mass. Now if balance cannot take place then some force is needed, and this is supplied by a force of motion measured by the product of the mass in pounds (weight in pounds divided by 32) and the change in feet of the velocity in feet per second which occurs during one second, the result being an equivalent force in pounds. Now let us suppose that a certain quantity, say 3 lbs. weight, of water is exposed in one place to a pressure of 20 lbs. over its surface, which is, say, 1 square inch, and at another place is exposed to the atmospheric pressure, which is nearly 15 lbs. per square inch. Then we have a column (not necessarily wholly, or even in part, vertical) 1 square inch cross-section, weighing 3 lbs., and acted on by a force of 20 — 15 = 5 lbs. Now to balance this an opposite force of 5 lbs. is needed (*i.e.*, if the water is not to move there must be, say, 20 lbs. air-pressure, or only 15 lbs. value for the other pressure), and this balance will be supplied, if not otherwise available, by a force of motion which, by our rule just given :—

$$\text{Mass} \times \text{acceleration} = \text{pounds of force};$$

$$\frac{3}{32} \times \text{acceleration} = 5;$$

$$\therefore \text{acceleration} = \frac{5 \times 32}{3} = 53\tfrac{1}{3} \text{ ft. per second};$$

i.e. : Such a mass of water, if still, would have at the end of the first second $53\tfrac{1}{3}$ ft. velocity per second; or, if already moving, would have increased its velocity by that amount.

Our next consideration is how area of the conduit and the quantity passing affects the velocity. Now if we take any point in the pipe and collect the quantity of water which passes in one second, measuring it in cubic feet, it is obviously the same as if we took a prism whose cross-section was the same as that of the pipe, and whose length in feet was the number of feet velocity per second (*i.e.*, as if such a prism were pushed through the pipe in a second), and we then get that :—Velocity in feet per second × cross-section at area in square feet of pipe = quantity in cubic feet passing per second.

Further, we notice that if the quantity passing through the whole pipe (whether it changes section or not) is constant, the quantity in the pipe everywhere must be constant. Hence the quantity flowing per second = velocity × area at one place = velocity at second place × area at second place.

This fact enables us to tell how the velocity will change if the area of the pipe changes (disregarding frictional losses), as obviously the velocity and area will change in inverse proportion. [It also provides us with a ready means of finding how much water is passing through a channel, as, if we note the velocity by the times at which floats are seen to cross certain points and measure the cross-sectional area of the stream at the same place, the product will give us the quantity, and this, multiplied by the total available head, is the work the stream can do.]

Next as to friction. This occurs in several ways:—

(1) By rubbing against the sides of the conduit.
(2) By eddies created at change of section and curvatures.
(3) By internal rubbing (" viscosity "). This last is usually negligible, being quite small.

In accordance with our general rule the friction in a system is most conveniently measured by taking the number of feet which is to be deducted from the available head.

As regards rubbing in the length of a pipe, experiment shows that the friction varies as the square of the velocity, as the length, and inversely as the depth; so that to find the loss we use the following rule:—

Loss of head in feet due to friction

$$= \cdot 0004 \times \frac{\text{length in feet}}{\text{diameter in feet}} \times (\text{velocity})^2 \text{ feet.}$$

As the loss is proportional to length, there will be a continuous decrease in the available head, which is known as the hydraulic gradient.

I give an illustration showing the hydraulic gradient right through a power system (fig. 2).

Next as to the loss at varying sections. Obviously there will be change in the velocities by our last rule but one; and taking the velocity head for each section by the expression in our first chapter

$$\frac{(\text{velocity})^2}{64},$$

the difference between these is the energy-loss by eddies in the water at this point.

Head loss by eddy at change of section

$$= \frac{[(\text{old velocity}) - (\text{new velocity})]^2}{64}.$$

Finally, loss by change of direction is best avoided by making all curves very easy and, as far as possible, continuous in direction—i.e., they should not unless it is impracticable to avoid it, have curvature alternately one way and then the other. The change of head at altering sections

B

can be utilised for suction purposes, as since total head is constant, if the velocity is much increased by reducing the section, the pressure head will decrease until it falls below the atmospheric. This is the principle of the jet pump.

Hydraulic mains must usually be designed to withstand great pressure, and there is a rule connecting the pressure with thickness as follows:—

Pull in material of section (lbs. per sq. in.)

$$= \frac{\text{pressure inside}}{\text{(lbs. per sq. in.)}} \; \frac{\text{(inside radius (ins.)}^2 + \text{(outside radius)}}{\text{(outside radius)}^2 - \text{(inside radius)}^2}$$

In fig. 2 I show the construction of a high-pressure joint consisting of two turned ends, one projecting and fitting into a recess in the other, with a ring of gasket filling a triangular groove, the whole bolted together by means of oval lugs cast on the ends of the pipes. For lesser pressures ordinary circular flanges on the ends of the pipe packed between with gasket ring and bolted will suffice.

There is also shown a valve to prevent pressure rising above a certain value as determined by the pressure which the loaded valve lever produces on the seating of the valve. When this is exceeded the water opens the valve (pulling down the lever and spindle) and escapes to waste.

Fig. 1 shows the general arrangement of the system in which use is made of water power for pressing purposes. We have the following series corresponding to that referred to in the "loss of energy diagram":—

(1) Pump, which raises water, giving it pressure energy. The work of the pump per stroke equals the weight of water which the pump barrel can contain in cubic feet, multiplied by the height to which it is raised if sent to a tank; or if to an accumulator, the equivalent height which water would have to produce the same pressure. This work (foot-pounds) multiplied by number of strokes divided by the time during which they are done (seconds), and again divided by 550, is the effective horse power of the pump. Or, again, the pressure in pounds per square inch in the steam cylinder × average area of piston × length of stroke in feet × number of strokes per second ÷ 550 = horse power of engine, which will be rather in excess of the pump's power on account of frictional loss.

Thus engine's work + friction and power absorbed in moving engine and pump's own parts = pump's work.

(2) Accumulator, which consists of a heavy weight (its construction is described later) balanced on the pressure water. This is kept at one fairly constant level by the pumps, as when it descends through drawing off the pressure water it restarts the steam engine, which it had previously stopped when it was raised to its determined level. The pressure which it produces equals the weight of the supported mass divided by the cross-sectional area of the column of water which supports it, and it is this pressure (pounds per square inch) which is used in the machinery.

The accumulator stores work to the amount of the weight of the moving mass (pounds) multiplied by the length of its stroke in feet, but of course this energy is constantly replenished by the pumps as it is drawn upon.

(3) Communication through intensifier, which increases the pressure in the inverse proportion of the areas of the pistons.

(4) Hydraulic press (described later), which brings the pressure to bear on that which is to be pressed. The amount of this pressure is (in the case illustrated of a downward acting pressure) equal to the weight of the moving part added to the product of the area in square inches of the piston (less the rod) and the pressure in pounds per square inch supplied by the intensifier. Work per stroke = this total pressure × length of stroke.

(5) Diminisher, for raising the ram when done with.

There will be frictional losses throughout the system due to the causes already mentioned, and hence we must minimise as much as possible the velocity in the pipes. This is the most important point to be noticed in all hydraulic machinery, as although it is extremely efficient for great pressures when distances are small, if the distances or arrangements are such that the velocity in the pipes is great the losses will also be considerable, in addition to which owing to the incompressibility of water, shocks will occur when the flow is suddenly stopped. The friction which occurs at the leather packings is also noteworthy. The following rule is fairly accurate :—

If the total pressure in pounds in the cylinder is multiplied by $^4/_{100}$ and divided by the diameter of the packed piston rod (or ram) in inches, the result is, in pounds, the force required to overcome friction. This multiplied by the stroke = work lost per stroke.

We will now consider the construction of presses in detail, and note the principles on which they depend.

CHAPTER III.

THE HYDRAULIC PRESS.

THIS apparatus, which owes its practical utility to the inventiveness of Bramah, consists essentially of a piston acted upon by water, and moving in a cylinder resembling faintly the cylinder of an ordinary steam engine. The pressure on the piston is communicated through a rod (very frequently the rod and piston form one cylindrical piece, termed a "ram ") to the place where the pressure is to be exerted for hoisting, packing, or other purpose. The pressure of the water has its origin in another contrivance (the pump), which arranges things in just the reverse way to the press—*i.e.*, an outside pressure (steam or hand) acts on a piston rod, through which it is communicated to water. This water entirely fills the communication between the two cylinders, and, seeing that water is practically incompressible, and also transmits (in virtue of this incompressibility and absence of internal friction) any pressure equally in all directions from each square inch of area with which the pump piston acts on the water, the pressure through the rod will be borne by the water and transmitted in equal measure to every other square inch of surface in the containing vessels.

Thus, pressure throughout system (while at rest or moving slowly) = total pressure on pump (or total weight of supported column of water from a tank, or total weight of supported water and load in the case of an accumulator) divided by the cross-sectional area of the piston (or ram in the "moving ram accumulator") = pressure on every 1 square inch of surface in the water-containing vessels.

(Incidentally, it follows that every pipe, joint, and cylinder must be able to stand this pressure. See previous rule connecting pressure inside and tension in the material of a pipe.)

This leads to the somewhat paradoxical result that a small pressure on a small area may produce elsewhere a great pressure on a great area, the only condition being that the proportion between the pressure and area (*i.e.*, the pressure in pounds per square inch) is constant. The apparent want of balance here is explained by the fact that the motion of the large area will be less than that of the small area in exactly the same proportion as the one area exceeds the other.

Hence we have the following balance of work :—

That pressure on one piston × its motion = total pressure on other piston × its motion.

Compare also *the balance* of pressures :—

Water pressure in pounds per square inch on one piston = water pressure in pounds per square inch on other piston.

In designing the press and accumulator we must, therefore, proportion the piston areas so that we get at the press the required length of stroke as compared with the accumulator stroke. (N.B.—The pump will not respond quickly enough to prevent the accumulator ram moving through part of its stroke due to drawing off the water.)

The construction of the press is usually as follows: A thick cast-steel cylinder of inside diameter rather larger than that of the ram (or exactly the same as that of the piston), and outside diameter rather in excess of that obtained from our thickness rule, bolted through projecting lugs to a concrete foundation, deep and wide enough to spread its weight over a sufficient bearing surface of soil. This cylinder is closed at one end, the other opening upwards or downwards according to the direction of the stroke. At the mouth a rebate is cut out from the bore which is there contracted to the exact size of the piston rod or ram, into which fits a circular ring of leather (section either H, U or L), so that the water pressure flattens it against the ascending or descending ram in its effort to escape, and the greater the pressure the less is the chance of escape. These rings are of compressed leather, and on them the efficiency of the pump largely depends. They do not last very long, and usually fail through the water bursting through a pore in the leather, making a pinhole. The water then escapes freely, and the leather must be renewed. To keep the leather in place a metal ring is fitted to it, and above this a gland (see illustration), which slides over the ram and is bolted down to the cylinder. The surface of the cylinder in the bore may have a gun-metal lining.

The ram or piston, being subject usually only to great pressure, can be of cast iron or cast steel, and is usually a plain solid or slightly hollow cylinder with the pressure end rounded off and the other end fitted by socket or bolted flange to the press plates. The latter are usually

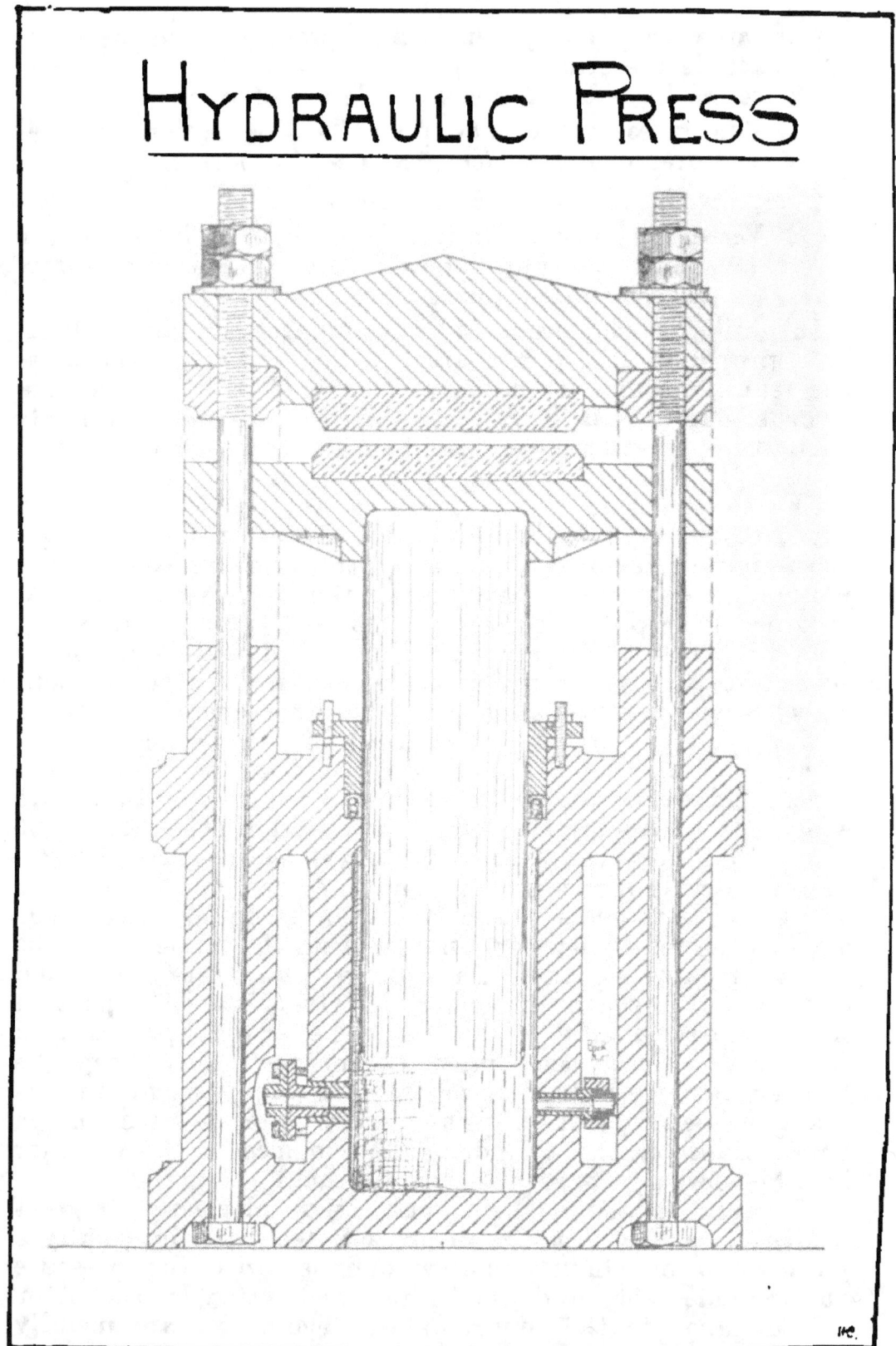

FIG. 3.—Hydraulic Press.

cast iron (but preferably steel) with either true faces or else dies of special form. They must be very rigid, and are usually fitted with slide blocks to pass between bars or over the surfaces of column bolts which connect the main cylinder with an upper frame bearing the top press plate. The essential throughout is great solidity and ability to resist compression (or in the column bolts an equal and opposite tension). The water connections are made by fitting screwed lining tube to the orifices into which the ends of the mains are screwed, with conical spigots and bolted down by flanges against flat surfaces on the cylinder. For small pressure an outside thread on the lining tube left projecting and a sound back nut connection with packing will suffice. (See fig. 3 for these details.) The jointing of the mains has already been described.

The *accumulator* is neither more nor less than a hydraulic press, in which energy is stored by the raising of a very heavily-loaded piston. There are two forms, one in which the ram moves and is supported on a column of water in the cylinder (which is fed from the pumps), and the other in which the ram is fixed and hollow, the load having within it a cylinder fitting over the ram: water enters by a central pipe in the ram, this being the supporting column. As the latter kind presents a smaller surface of water, a greater pressure in pounds per square inch is obtained. The weight consists of massive section castings supported on a press plate (no top plate is, of course, necessary), or a large heavy container, which is filled with scrap iron or heavy clinker until sufficient pressure is obtained by the rule: Total load on accumulator in pounds ÷ cross-sectional area of the supporting column of water = water pressure in pounds per square inch.

We can in this way get pressures of 2 tons or more per inch, which, acting in a press with a ram of, say, 20 square inches, gives a total pressure there of 40 tons. With intensifiers or compound presses we can get hundreds, or even thousands, of tons, the motions being, however, correspondingly reduced.

The accumulator acts as a steam governor by raising the counter balance of a weighted lever steam throttle valve when its top level is reached, and, as a further precaution, there is usually a safety catch on the guide bars between which the load is steadied, which will, if a certain level is exceeded (by failure of the valve control), release the pressure water to waste.

As previously mentioned, the losses in an accumulator are small, but can be taken in detail as follows :—

1. *Friction at Packing Leather.*—This can be minimised by sensitive pumps, so that the accumulator does not move much.

FIG. 5.—Accumulator.

2. *Friction in Guide Bars.*—It is usually impossible to so exactly balance the moving load that no lateral pressure occurs, in addition to which there will be some cohesion, and also some viscosity in the lubricant. This is minimised as before by keeping the load still.

3. *Loss of Pressure at Connection with Main.*—This will be great if the velocity of the water is great, as previously explained ; but we must not have a great velocity. This is the most important source of loss, but should not exceed 3 per cent of the stored energy.

4. *Loss Due to Escape of Pressure Water.*—This, of course, can only be avoided by careful fitting and good leathers.

The press losses are similar in nature, and reducible by the same means. There is also loss in the pressure of waste water, which has pressure from the descent of the ram. Unless this can be utilised in smaller machines, or returned in the system at some point of low pressure, the loss from this cause can only be minimised by reducing the water space as much as possible. All valves should be opened slowly, so that the water may not lose energy by sudden change of velocity. This loss is important, both from the point of view of maximum efficiency and also more particularly in regard to fracture of pipes and the leakage of joints. This is the weak point of the hydraulic system, and there must be no leakage of pressure water anywhere.

CHAPTER IV.

APPLICATIONS OF PRESS.

THE applications of the press are now exceedingly numerous and important, so that space forbids a very detailed discussion of them. The chief uses, however, are :

1. Pressing machinery for welding, forging, cotton packing, extraction of oils, brick and stone making, pipe making, cable insulating, and steel compressing.

2. Hoisting machinery for lifts, guns, and cranes.

3. Recoil mechanism for guns.

4. Slewing mechanism for guns, cranes, and machinery.*

The first class consists essentially of the Bramah press, as described, either with intensifiers or compound cylinders and rams, so that enormous pressures can be produced. Working pressures of upwards of 3 tons per square inch are in common use ; the press cylinders being about 14 in. or 15 in. diameter, and the metal upwards of 3 in. thick. The tensile stresses produced in the metal work out to about 25 to 30 tons per square inch, which can be withstood by good cast steel. The presses may act upwards or downwards, according to convenience and the pressure required. If the ram is lifted on the working stroke, its weight, including that of the top plate or "platen," acts against the water pressure, thus reducing it. On the other hand, it descends automatically when the water is allowed to escape. Downward-acting presses add this weight to the water pressure, but need extra water to lift them again. This is sometimes accomplished by a hand pump, seeing that only a small pressure (= weight of ram and platen ÷ area of lifting cylinder in which it rests) is needed. Many convenient arrangements have been, and can be, devised by having multiple presses, which bring additional rams into operation as the need for greater pressure occurs.

As an example of the manner in which hydraulic power can be economically employed in compound presses, we can have a cast-steel frame containing three (or more) cylinders

---

* I am indebted to Messrs. Fielding and Platt for several photographs of Hydraulic Presses applied to different purposes.

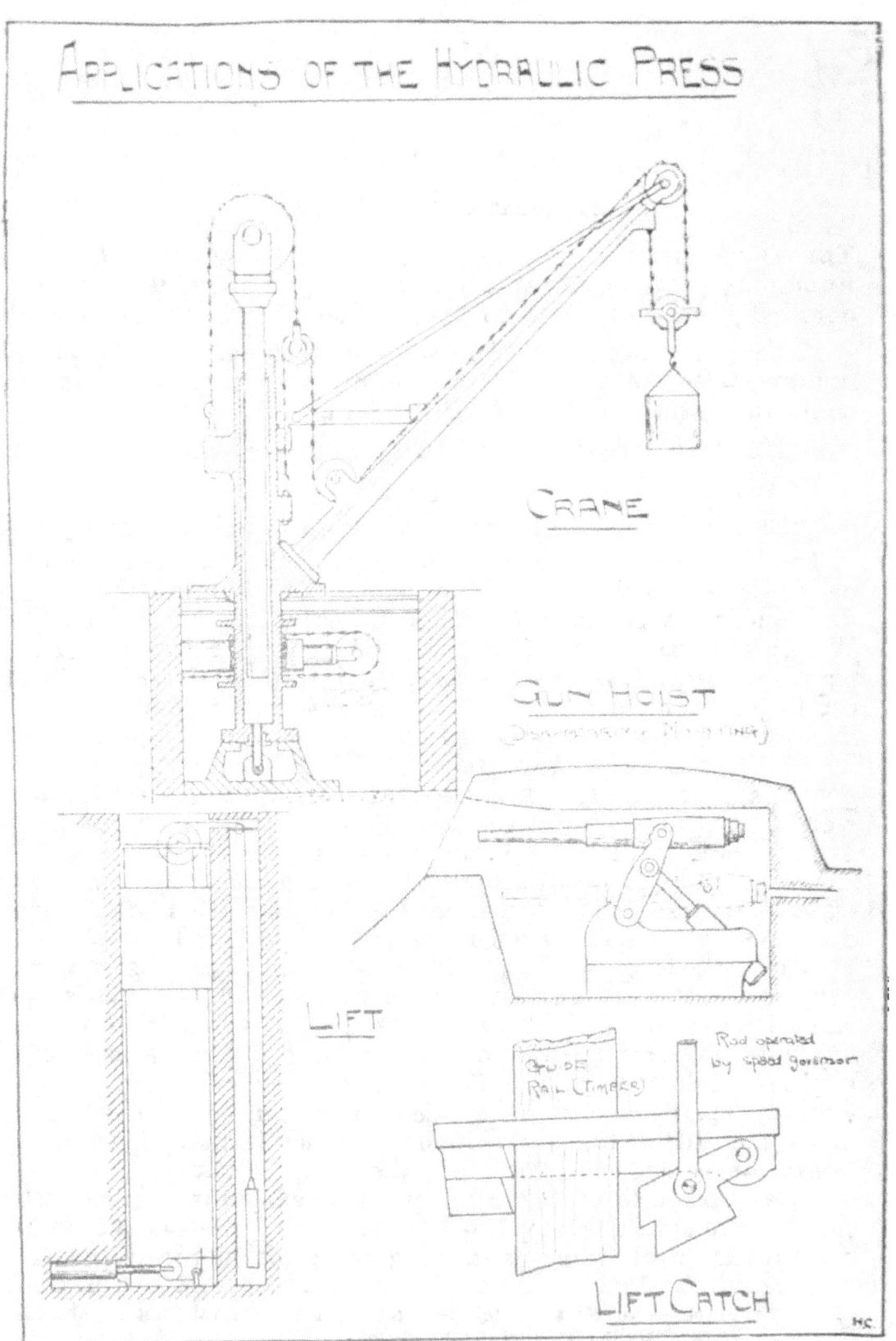

APPLICATIONS OF THE HYDRAULIC PRESS

CRANE

GUN HOIST

LIFT

GUIDE RAIL (TIMBER)

Rod operated by speed governor

LIFT CATCH

FIG. 6.

of the same or varying sizes. On the commencement of the stroke water is admitted to one cylinder, and lifts the platen and with it all the rams, the water being supplied to the other cylinders by inward opening valves from some convenient source of supply. When the height is reached at which great pressures are required the valves admitting pressure water to the other cylinders are opened, and we have all three acting upon the platen with a force corresponding to the combined areas of the rams used.

One point in connection with hydraulic presses is of some importance, especially as regards lifts, viz.: If the ram, with its load, is heavy, and when it is in the cylinder it is immersed in water, the pressure required to raise it

Fig. 7.—Plate Bending Machine.

increases as it leaves the water. This arises from the fact that over and above the applied pressure there is, when the ram is immersed, a pressure of "flotation," due to the reaction of the water which it displaces, so that while in the water the net weight of the ram is: Absolute weight — weight of water displaced, but as it rises this increases up to the absolute weight. The greatest difference producible in this way is cross-sectional area of ram in square feet × stroke in feet × 62·5 lbs.

Wherever the work to be done is not against a very great resistance, but through a very considerable distance, so that both a large range of motion and comparative rapidity is needed, it is customary to fix a sheave block to the head of the press ram, and a chain running over this multiplies the motion, at the same time decreasing the force exerted in the inverse proportion. (It must, however, be clearly

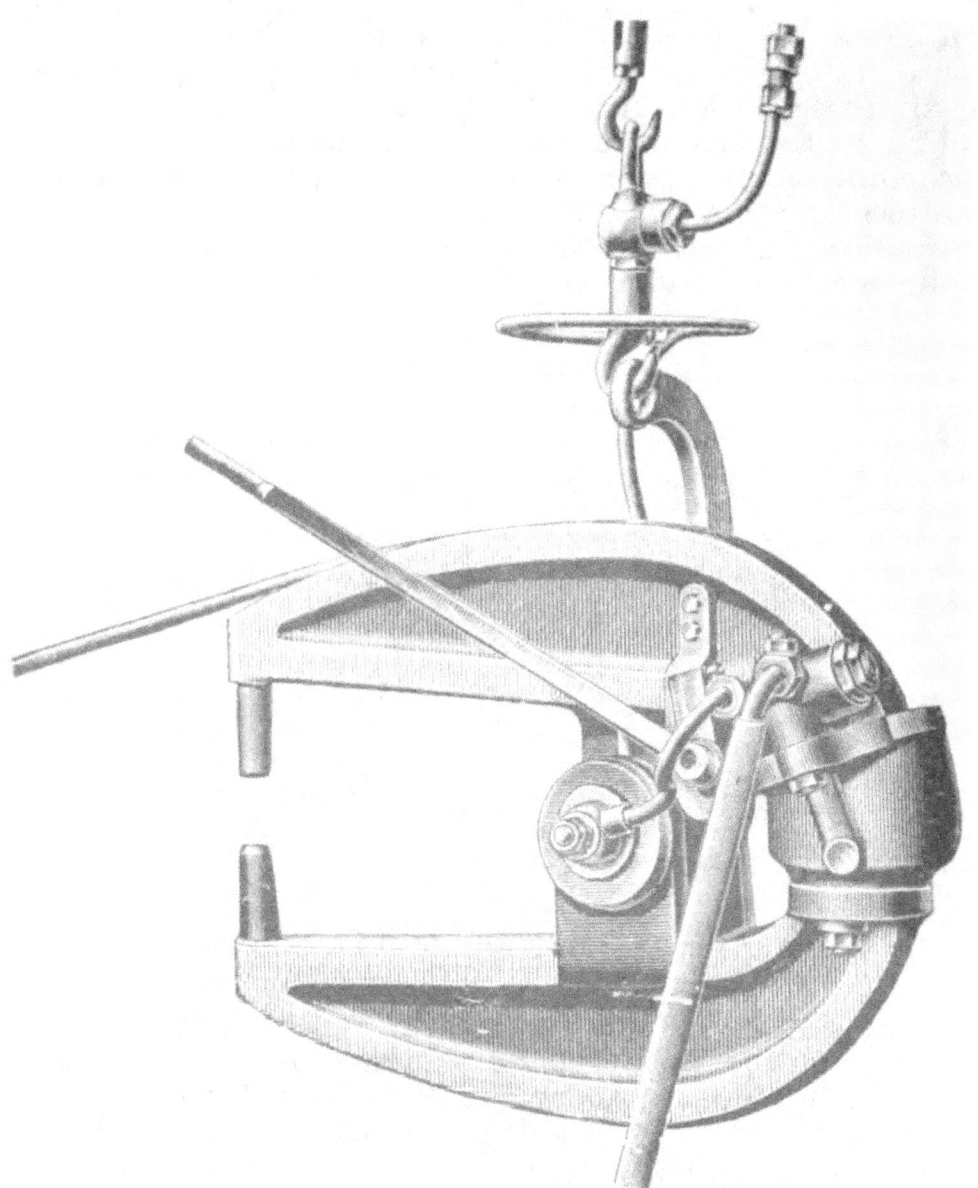

FIG. 8.—Portable Riveter with Hanger.

understood that a large part of the force will be absorbed in overcoming the friction at the pulley journals, in bending and stretching the chain, so that there is less economy of work than in a direct-acting press.) A very good example of this is seen in the Armstrong type of crane, of which I give an illustration (fig. 11). The introduction of this has to a great extent revolutionised the loading and unloading of ships. In connection with this appliance we have a very

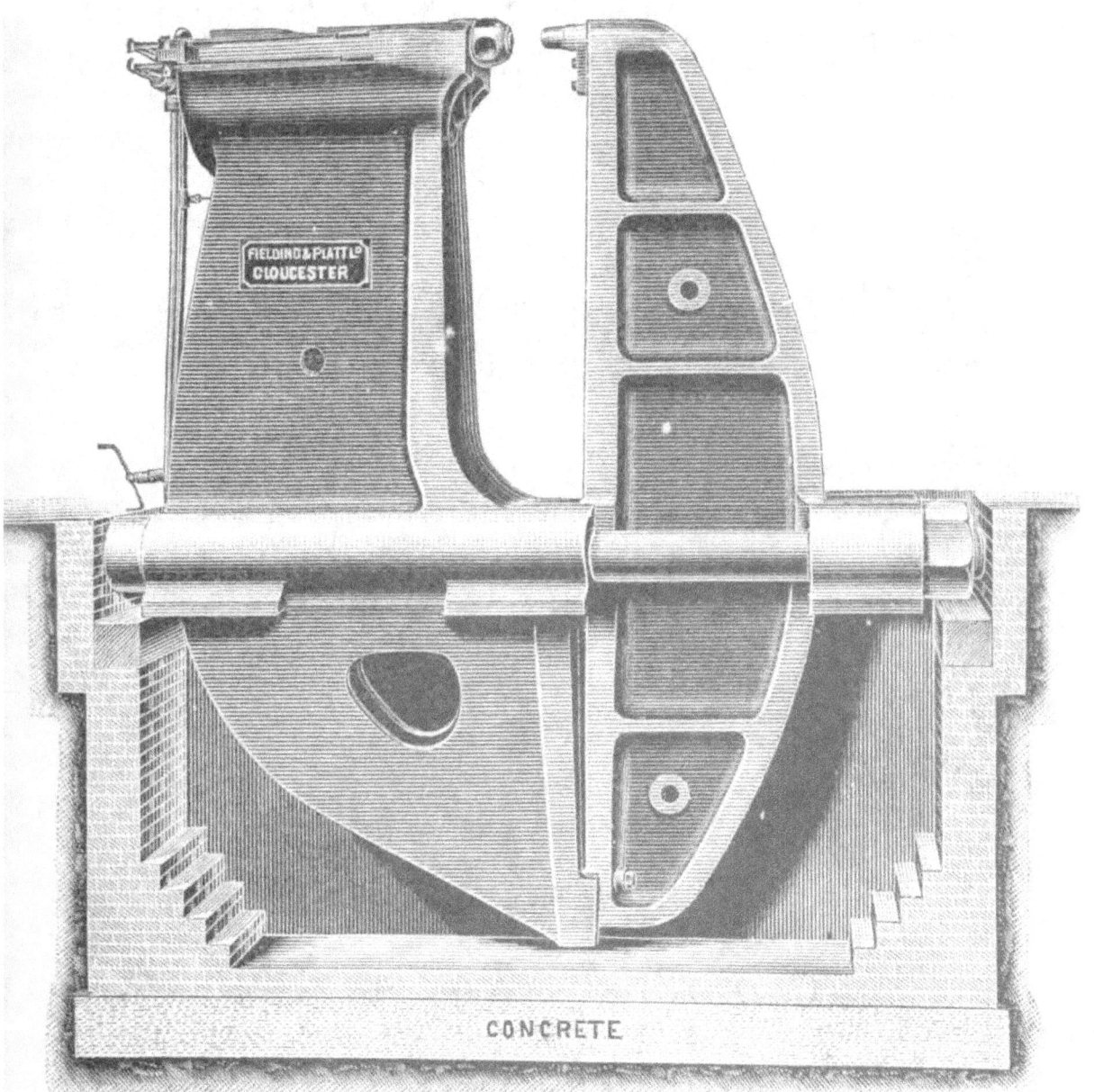

Fig. 9. – Stationary Riveter.

interesting and economical arrangement of the press on the differentiated principle. The cylinder has a close-fitting piston, upon which pressure water acts from the accumulator and pump ; at the back of the piston the rod or ram is fitted, and the pressure water is also admitted to this side, so that the actual total pressure on the ram is the accumulator pressure per square inch multiplied by the area of the piston. The advantage of this is that the water behind the rod is returned to the pumps (being at the same or slightly greater pressure per square inch), and so is economised.

Such a cylinder is usually fitted horizontally in a cavity prepared for it in the ground, and arranged so that its

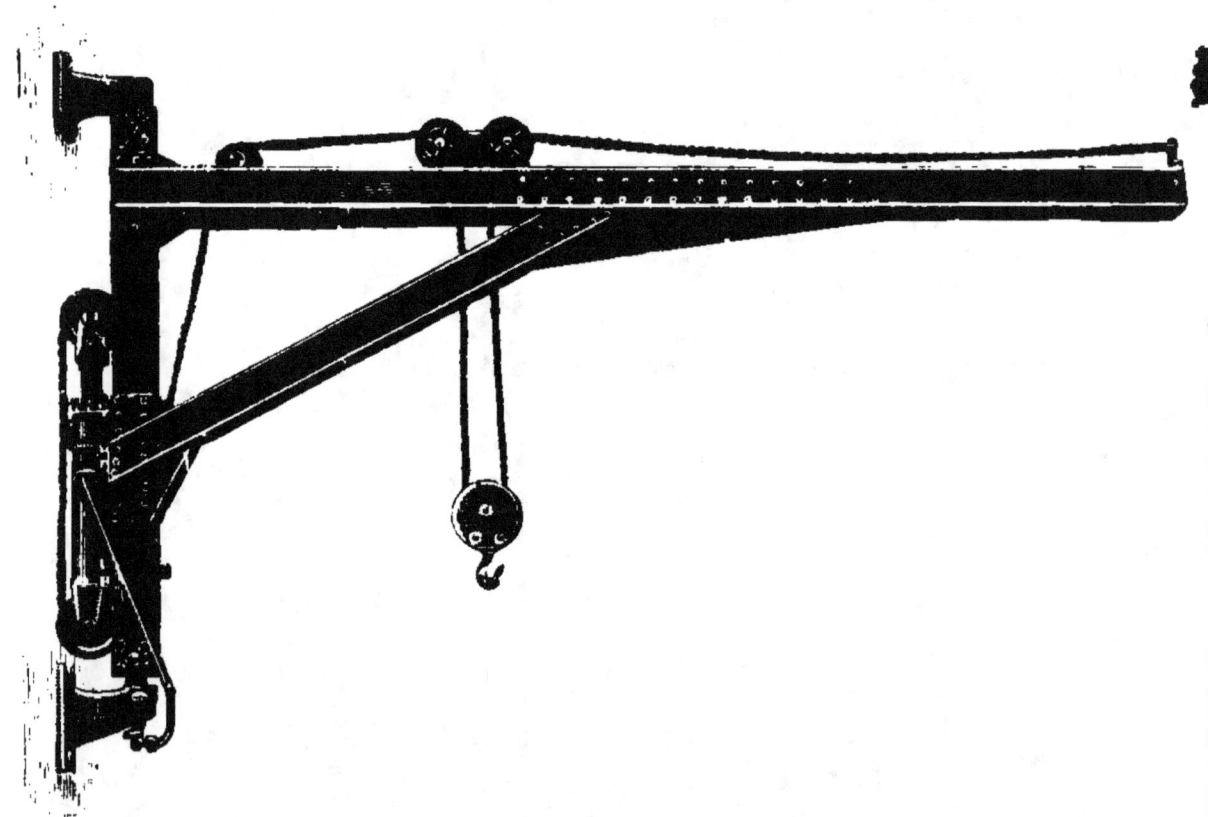

Fig. 10.—Wall Crane.

chain is fed over another sheave into the central standard of the crane, from which it goes over the jib sheave to the crane hook. An alternative arrangement is to have the hydraulic cylinder fixed within the crane standard, the ram acting up or down, and its motion transmitted by chain gearing as before. To give the crane horizontal rotation another cylinder is usually provided, with similar chain gearing, which acts upon a drum forming part of the crane standard. We have thus controlled by two (c.

at the most three) simple lever valves a crane capable of
lifting many tons. The greatest advantage lies in the fact
that the motion can be stopped at any instant with the
greatest ease, and on account of the multiplying gear is
not necessarily very slow. Thus a ram velocity of 10 ft.
per minute by chain gearing may be increased to 40 ft. per
minute—(remember that guide pulleys do not alter the
velocity ratio)—the actual pull being decreased in ratio to

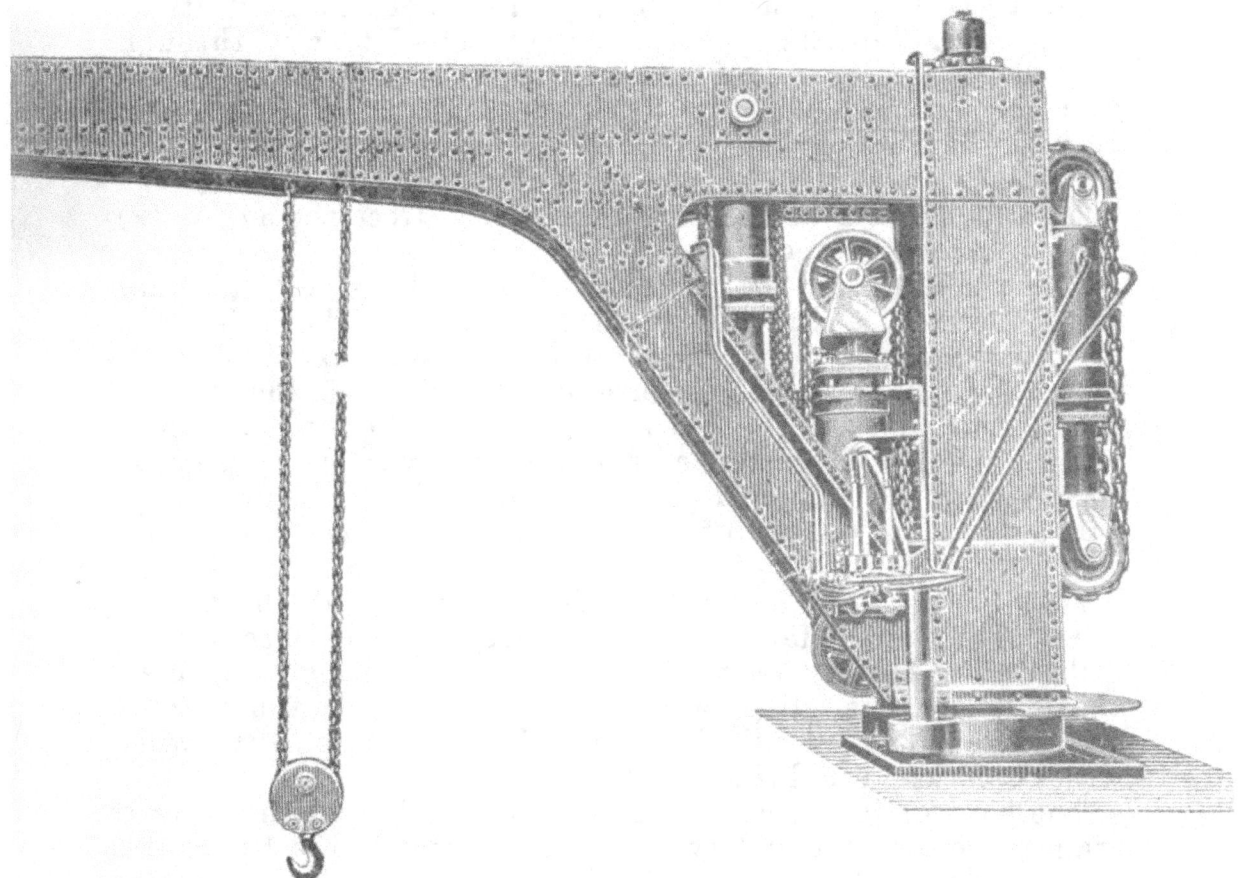

FIG. 11.—6-ton Crane.

the ram pressure by a fraction less than one-fourth, according to the efficiency of the gearing.

Another very ingenious application of the press is to lead-
pipe manufacture. Molten lead is admitted from a large
melting tank into a receptacle in the platen of a press, and
this is pushed on to a hollow ram. Fixed to the platen in
the receptacle and concentric with the ram is a rod, the
diameter of which equals the inside diameter of the pipe

C

required. The inside diameter of the hollow ram is equal to the outside diameter of the required pipe, so that the space between the rod and the ram into which it fits has an equal cross-sectional area to that required in the lead pipe. The platen in its ascent compresses the lead, and there are only three means of escape for it : one back to the melting tank, one past the ram packing, and one through the annular space between the rod and the ram. The first escape is prevented by increasing the head of molten lead or by a valve or by disconnection ; the second by good fitting and packing ; so that the lead is compelled to rise through the space and come off the end of the rod, having been compressed and cooled by a water jacket to a solid state. It emerges from the other end of the ram and is coiled upon a drum.

Hydraulic lifts are of two kinds, (1) direct-acting, or (2) rope or chain geared.

The direct-acting lift is raised by a long vertical ram which bears the lift cage upon its platen. The objections to this method are great. Considerable excavation is necessary, the loss of pressure by flotation of the ram is great, and also, if the cylinder cracks, leathers fail, or a valve bursts and water escapes, there may be a serious accident by the sudden fall of the ram, which, being heavy, will gain much energy of motion, and so cause great shock when stopped.

In all lifts there must be safety catches, which, in the event of a sudden fall from any cause, seize into the guide rails or some other part of the fixed construction. One of these catches is illustrated, and there are innumerable varieties ; but they will frequently fail to act, chiefly owing to lack of use and lubrication.

The geared lift is very similar in its design to the geared crane. The most usual type is that in which the hydraulic cylinder is at the base of the lift well, and the steel-wire rope or chain passes over pulley-wheel gearing up to a large wheel fixed at the head of the well, so that the rope will on the other side descend centrally and suspend the lift cage. The illustration shows the ram in tension during the ascent, but compression is far more usual. It is usual in both types of lift to counterbalance with a weight or small hydraulic accumulator (termed a balance), so that the majority of the energy stored in raising the cage is not lost at each ascent. Thus the actual energy used is only that required to overcome friction and raise passengers.

If, as frequently happens. there are as many passengers descending as ascending, the expenditure is even less.

For this reason the hydraulic lift is the most economical type yet known.

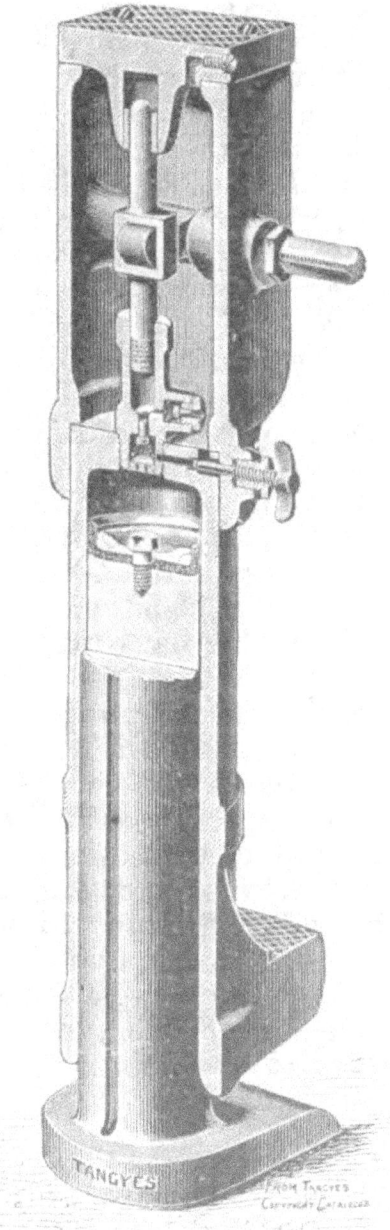

Fig. 12.—Hydraulic Jack.

A very convenient and useful appliance is the hydraulic jack, which consists of a fixed ram (with a cup leather on top). The cylinder, which is the lifting part of the mechanism, consists of two receptacles for water, one between the cylinder and the ram leather and one in the head. The two are in communication by means of a downward-opening valve, through which water is forced by a small plunger operated by a lever moving a cam working in a slot in the plunger. When the lever is moved downward, its motion being transferred through a spindle in the cylinder upon which is the cam referred to. The cam (which is on the same side of the spindle as the handle of lever) presses down the plunger, and this, which is hollow, takes in water from the upper receptacle through an inward-opening valve and presses it through the before-mentioned downward valve into the lower receptacle, causing pressure on the fixed ram. The ratio of the pressures is in the inverse proportion of the areas of the plunger and ram, which, taking into account the advantage given by the lever, enables hand pressure to raise loads of 1 to 10 tons.

See photograph of one of Messrs. Tangye's jacks.

A similar arrangement, with a frame and specially-made jaws, serves for riveting, punching, and shearing plates.

Hydraulic recoil buffers for artillery consist of cylinders fixed to the gun frame, in which move pistons rigidly fixed to the gun. The fore and back parts of the cylinder are connected with a pipe in which is a valve. Hence, when the gun is fired and recoils, it moves the pistons, displacing water (the cylinders are always full) from rear to fore part, the flow being controllable by the valve. The friction in the pipe caused by change of section, and any further friction which may be imparted at will by the valve, serves to absorb the kinetic energy of the gun and transform it into eddy friction of the water, which is dissipated as heat.

Another important application to modern artillery is the disappearing mounting, where we have a ram acting directly on to a lever which forms the gun mount, and raises it and the gun together to the firing level and lowers it again when fired.

CHAPTER V.

RUNNING WATER AND WATER WHEELS.

WE have hitherto confined our attention to pressure machines, and must now pass to those appliances which utilise the kinetic energy (*i.e.*, energy of motion of water). While reminding the student of the manner in which this energy of motion results from the liberation of potential and pressure energy, it is necessary to point out the effects of such energy of motion upon resistances opposed to the flow.

The measure of the energy, as will be remembered, is—

$$\frac{(\text{velocity in feet per second})^2}{64} = \text{per lb. of water ;}$$

so that if we know the weight of the water moving and its velocity, it is an easy matter to find the energy of motion. This, *in toto*, is the work which the water can do. If divided by time (*i.e.*, taken at so many feet per second), the result is the " power " or rate at which work can be done.

I have previously referred to the velocity produced by the action of a force on water. Now I must speak of the force produced by the alteration of an existing velocity.

The quantity which is obtained by multiplying weight in pounds ÷ 32 into the velocity in feet per second is called *momentum*. The change of *momentum* in feet per second is equal to the force in pounds which occurs as the result of changing velocity. Thus, if 1 lb. of water travelling at 10 ft. per second is stopped dead in *one second*, a force is exerted on the obstacle $= \frac{1}{32} \times 10 = \frac{5}{16}$ lb. If it occurred in two seconds, the force would be $\frac{5}{32}$ lb., and so on. We thus get the general result—

$$\frac{\text{weight in lbs.} \times \text{velocity (ft. per sec.)}}{32 \times \text{time in secs. of stopping}} = \text{force exerted in stopping.}$$

If it so happens that the water is thrown back by the shock, so as to get a backward velocity (this will depend on

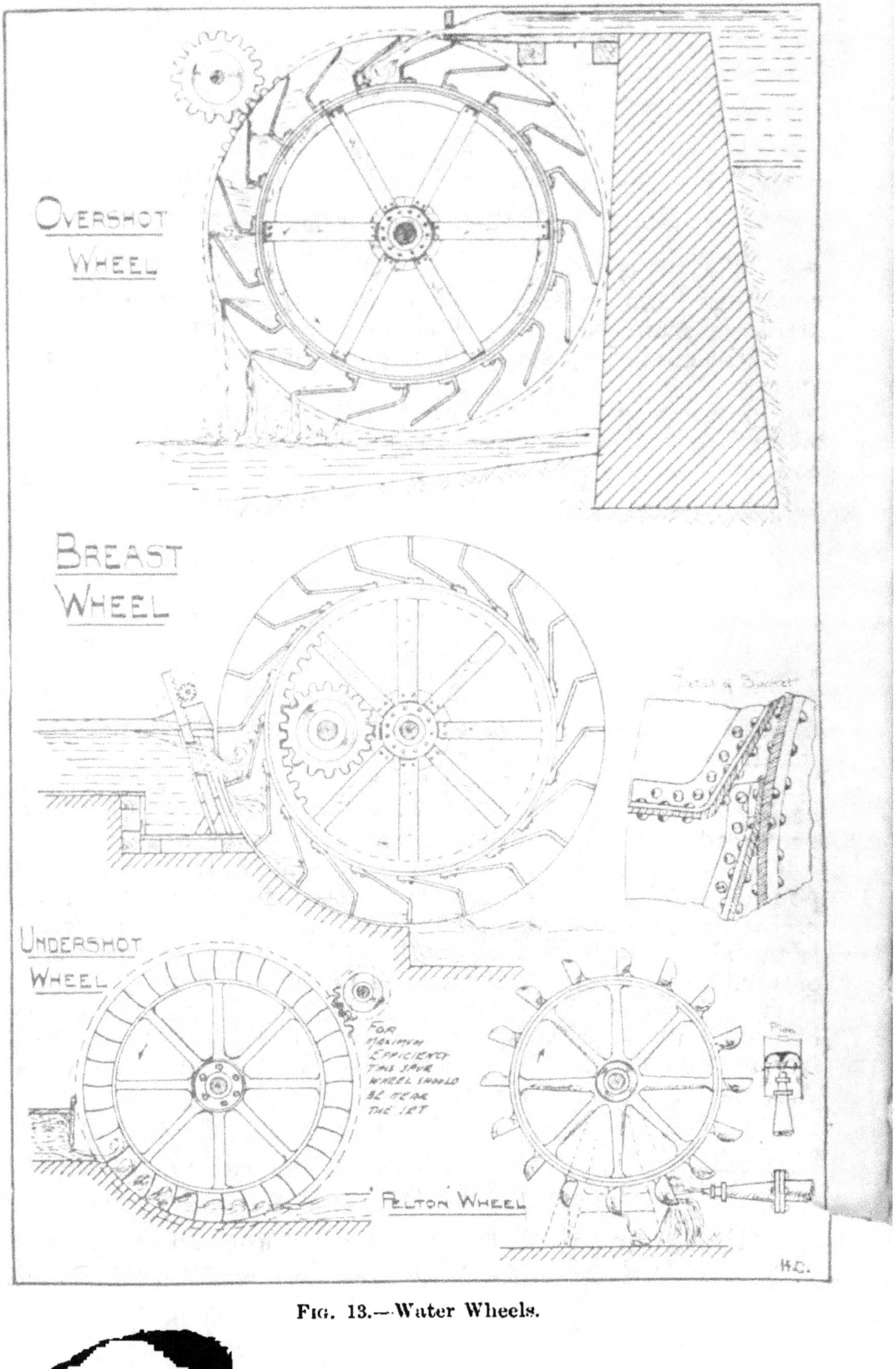
OVERSHOT WHEEL
BREAST WHEEL
UNDERSHOT WHEEL
FOR MAXIMUM EFFICIENCY THIS SPUR WHEEL SHOULD BE NEAR THE JET
PELTON WHEEL
Plan
H.C.

Fig. 13.—Water Wheels.

the form of the surface of the obstacle), then the total change of momentum

$$= \frac{\text{weight (lbs.)} \times (\text{velocity of approach} + \text{velocity of return})}{32},$$

which, divided by the time in which it occurs. gives the total force exerted by the obstacle against the water. This force can be, and is in the case of water wheels and turbines, used to do work.

If the water flows continuously, and all its energy of motion is absorbed in moving the obstacle, it follows that during each second the whole momentum of the water is converted, so that we get the great rule relating to these machines, viz., the momentum of the water taken in pounds and feet per second is the force exerted on the mechanism. We must, however, only consider the *relative* velocity of the water to the wheel vane.

Seeing that this momentum is the equivalent of a force, we can find the work which the water does per second by multiplying this momentum by the distance through which the point struck by the water moves per second. If this is at right angles to the flow of the water and none of the energy is wasted, the velocity of the point will be half that of the water; so we get a further rule regarding these machines :—

If the "vanes" are radial (*i.e.*, along a radius of the wheel), and the water strikes tangentially (*i.e.*, at right angles to a radius), the work per second = momentum of the water × velocity of the water (referred to vane) in feet per second.

Or, more completely,

$$\frac{\text{Gallons per sec.} \times 10 \text{ lbs.}}{32} \times (\text{velocity ft. per sec.})^2$$

= work in foot-pounds per second.

(This divided by 550 = theoretical horse power.)

In the early types of water wheel we have three varieties :—

1. The overshot.
2. The breast.
3. The undershot.

The names, of course, refer to the position of the water jet which drives the wheel. In nearly all cases the stream above the wheel (the head water) is conducted to the wheel through a properly-formed channel, and is dammed up by a weir, so that the surface of the overflowing water is at the same level as the part of the wheel upon which it is to act. The water then passes either (1) over, (2) down, or (3) under the vanes of the wheel on the head-water side, and leaves the wheel by another channel (the "tail race").

The energy of the wheel is entirely kinetic, and is to be found by the rule—

$$\frac{(\text{Force lbs.}) \times (\text{velocity of circumference ft. per sec })}{550} = \text{H.P.}$$

Or,

$$\frac{(\text{Force} \times \text{radius}) \times 6\cdot28 \times \text{revolutions per sec.}}{550} = \text{H.P.}$$

All this is supplied by the energy of motion or pressure possessed by the water, which arises from two causes :—

1. Velocity of approach in the head water.

2. Distance fallen from weir before striking vane [velocity = square root of (fall in feet × 64)]. (Overshot and breast wheels use chiefly the pressure due to weight.)

In designing a wheel to make use of an existing stream, we then have to consider three things :—

1. The quantity of water passing in a second.

2. The velocity of approach to the point at which the wheel can be placed.

3. The relative levels of the head water, wheel spindle, and tail race.

Upon the first and last will depend the type of wheel adopted.

To find the quantity of water passing we observe the velocity by means of light floats, noticing the time which they take to pass certain points in the stream, so that

$$\frac{\text{Distance between the two points (feet)}}{\text{Time, in secs., in passing from one to other}} = \text{velocity in ft. per sec.}$$

This multiplied by the mean cross-sectional area of the stream in square feet gives the quantity in cubic feet which passes every second.

To find the energy which this will impart to the wheel we multiply the weight in pounds (*i.e.*, cubic feet × 62½) by the fall in feet which it can get before striking the wheel vanes, and if there is any considerable velocity of approach, we also multiply the

$$\text{weight in lbs.} \times \frac{\text{velocity}^2}{64}$$

The sum of these two quantities—

$$\{\text{Weight} \times (\text{fall} + v^2/64)\} = \text{total energy of the water.}$$

If the wheel is properly made it will have an efficiency (*i.e.*, ratio of actual to theoretical power) of upwards of 50 per cent, so that this result, divided by 550 to convert to horse power, and again divided by 2, will give the effective horse power of the wheel. In considering the work to be done by the wheel (such as mill grinding, pumping, etc.), we must also allow for loss of the power absorbed into the gearing. This is frequently a considerable item, especially when timber shafting is used.

It will be fairly obvious that the type of wheel adopted depends on the nature of the supply. If we can get great velocity of approach with but little fall, then the undershot type will be used. If there is very little velocity but considerable head, the overshot wheel is preferable. If there is a fair velocity and also some head available, then a breast wheel will be preferable.

A great disadvantage with the overshot wheel is that the tail water does not clear readily, having no forward velocity when it leaves the wheel, and in this respect the breast and undershot wheels are preferable.

The form of the bucket or vane is a matter of great importance, and upon it largely depends the efficiency of the wheel. The angle at which the water meets the surface of the bucket will determine the relative velocity of the circumference and water. If the vanes are radial, then either the wheel moves with half the velocity of the water or energy is wasted, because if vane moves with nearly same velocity as the water there will be no pressure on it, and if its velocity is less than half the water will be thrown back. This form will obviously not retain the water after moving through a right angle, and so is unsuitable for over-shot or breast wheels, which depend largely for their efficiency on the water being suspended in the buckets and transferring their potential energy as kinetic in descent down the wheel.

If the vane is inclined towards the approaching water, the velocity of the wheel circumference can be more than half that of the water, just in the proportion that the deviation from the radial form bears to the slope of the vane, thus :—

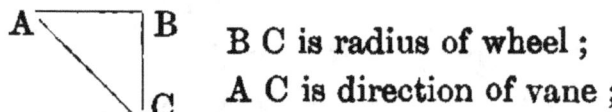

B C is radius of wheel ;

A C is direction of vane ;

$\dfrac{AB}{AC}$ is proportion of velocity gained.

We have also to remember that the water must be retained in some of the buckets during its descent, so that the capacity of these particular buckets must be sufficient (taking into account their velocity) to contain nearly all the water which passes through the stream.

Next must be considered the manner in which the water leaves the wheel. It will do so in the case of water wheels from the point at which it entered, on account of the changing position of the vane ; but in turbines, as we shall see, the angle of the vane at leaving is very important. The only thing necessary in a water wheel is, then, that the drum upon which the vanes are fixed shall be entirely covered, and have projecting flanges, so that each vane, with the drum and flanges, forms a bucket, or, if of metal, the vanes shall be bent at the back and sides to form a container. All this part of the wheel is termed "shrouding."

In the case of breast wheels where there is no velocity of approach to be considered, the vane should be directed upwards, so that the water falls (through an aperture in the upper trough) into the bucket, and remains there until it reaches the bottom of the wheel. They are always fed above the centre line.

The bottom of the bucket should be rounded, or else there will be considerable additional eddy friction.

In undershot wheels the vanes are, as in the overshot wheels, directed towards the flowing water, but seeing that this approaches the lower tangent of the circle, the buckets

FIG. 14.—Pelton Wheel.

must be reversed as compared with those of the overshot position.

The same rule as to comparative velocities of circumference and water applies to breast and undershot wheels.

The wheels used now are generally constructed of steel, with curved buckets, cast-steel spokes fixed to a central boss, which again is keyed to a supporter shaft. A toothed wheel gears with a toothed crown on the water wheel and runs on the driving shaft. The latter is properly supported in plummer blocks at both sides of the waterway. The power is transmitted through bevel gearing to the mechanism within a house or shed.

In the older type of wheel the construction is frequently of timber throughout, and the efficiency is smaller. These wheels usually turn out upwards of 25 per cent of the water power supplied to them, whereas the best modern wheels approach 70 per cent, or even more.

The *Pelton* wheel, of which the two essential features are double cusp-formed buckets, which throw back (or, rather, down) water striking them (or, rather, *one*) from a nozzle, is in considerable favour with hydraulic engineers, and its efficiency approaches 90 per cent. (See Gilbert Gilkes' photograph, fig. 14.)

The construction is very simple, and the apparatus is easily fixed in any position to which pressure water can be conveyed by a main. The small size of the wheel and its high efficiency recommend it strongly.

The water wheel for power supply is rapidly being displaced by the turbine, which is, in fact, a water wheel of much smaller size and greater convenience and efficiency.

There are considerable losses (apart from the inconvenience) resulting from wasted water in the water wheel, and these are greatly minimised in the turbine, which forms the subject of our next chapter.

CHAPTER VI.

TURBINES.

A TURBINE is a water wheel of high velocity and through water passage.

There are two types:—

1. The reaction turbine, which always runs full, and uses pressure and momentum.

2. The impulse turbine, which takes a smaller supply of water, does not necessarily run full, and uses momentum only.

Each type can be again subdivided into three classes:—

1. Inward flow, where the water enters the outer circumference of the wheel and leaves at the inner.

2. Outward flow, where the water enters at the inner circumference and leaves at the surface.

3. Axial flow, where the water enters and leaves parallel to the axis of rotation.

A characteristic feature of the turbine as compared with the water wheel is that the water usually acts upon the whole circumference of the wheel (or "rotor") instead of one part. The results are a much more continuous and regular turning effect and a smaller wheel. We must have, however, some means of conveying the water to the circumference of the rotor, and this is obtained by forming a chamber concentric with the wheel into which the water is led, passing on to the rotor through fixed guides.

The most important question connected with the design of turbines lies in the correct direction of the guides and vanes. We have to consider four angles:—

1. That at which the water enters the guides having regard to its direction of approach.

HYDRAULIC TURBINES

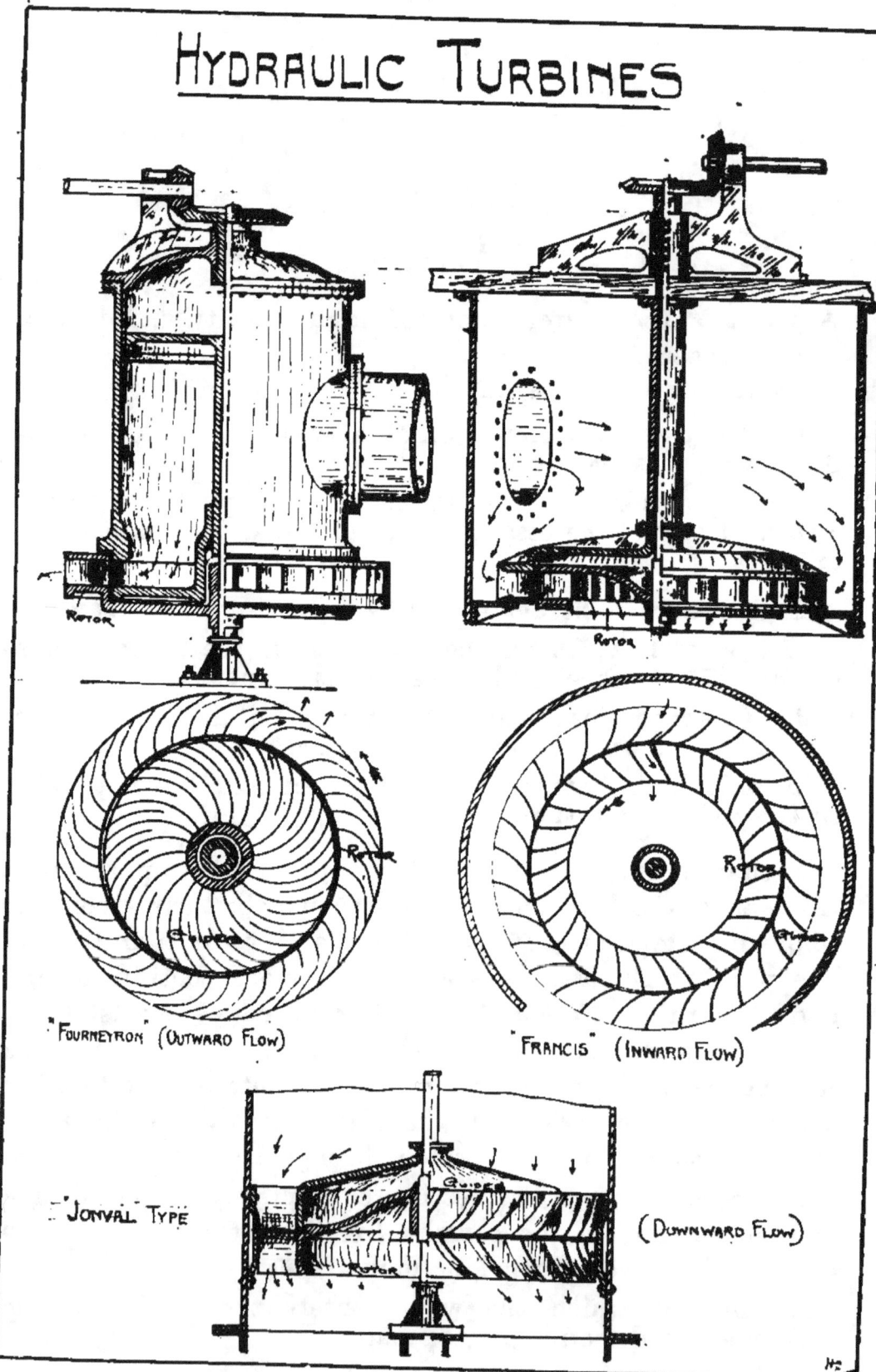

"FOURNEYRON" (OUTWARD FLOW)

"FRANCIS" (INWARD FLOW)

"JONVAL" TYPE

(DOWNWARD FLOW)

FIG. 15.

2. That at which the water leaves the guides at the moment of entering the rotor, in view of the velocity of the wheel circumference.

3. That at which the vanes of the rotor meet the water as it issues from the guides, having regard to the relative velocities of the vane and the water, and also the turning effect which the water is required to produce.

4. That at which the water leaves the rotor, noticing that a certain quantity must pass through the wheel in a certain time, and that its direction and velocity at the moment of leaving must be such as to cause the least possible resistance to the wheel.

It is necessary here to refer back to the manner in which the vanes of the water wheel were to be directed towards the water, and also to notice that :--

1. The guides turn the water into a given direction.

2. The vanes must oppose the maximum useful resistance to the flow of the water, having regard to the velocity and work of the wheel.

3. The exit from the vane is to guide the water away with the minimum velocity in the direction of rotation.

The velocity of the vanes would be the same as that of the water if at right angles to the direction of flow when this is the result of pressure, and more if the vanes are inclined towards that direction. It will be less if the vane is inclined backwards, and always in the proportion in which the deviation from a radius bears to the length of vane in which such deviation is made (or, in trigonometric language, the " cosine of the angle between vane and circumference ").

Hence we have the following general rules as to the direction of guides and vanes :—

INWARD-FLOW TURBINE.

Water enters chamber radially, and the guides must therefore be nearly radial at the outer edge. They will then curve *gently* in, and deliver at a slight angle with the inner circumference (see illustration). The vane angle there will be at right angles to the guide exit (or inclined towards or from it according as its velocity is to be more or

FIG. 17.—Vortex Turbine.

less than the water). There will then be in the vane an easy reflex curvature, so that the water leaves the inner circumference of the wheel in such a direction backwards that combining its required radial (*i.e.*, *through*) velocity with the velocity of that circumference there is no tendency to move with the wheel, thus :—

A B = velocity of inner circumference;
A C = radial velocity of water ;
ABC = angle of vane exit.

It will be noticed how the through velocity affects the work of the turbine.

OUTWARD-FLOW TURBINE.

In discussing the previous type the essential principles of all turbine design are described, and to apply them to the reverse flow is a simple matter. The water enters near the axis of the wheel in a fixed casing with easy water passage, the inner angle of the guides being such that the water enters them in the direction of its motion. If the chamber is circular, and is supplied by a pipe entering tangentially, the guide vane angle at entrance must be nearly tangential, but more usually there is a radial flow and entrance. Passing by easy curvature to the outer circumference of the fixed chamber, the leaving angle is again nearly tangential, and the water will now have to strike the moving vanes at right angles to their entrance angle (as before, the angle may be more or less than a right angle, according to the relative speed required). By curvature (sometimes reflex) the water leaves the vane with only radial velocity at the angle of exit, being sloped backwards to obtain this result, as before.

AXIAL-FLOW TURBINE.

In this case the revolving portion is above or below the fixed part, and the water enters vertically. The guide blades must therefore be vertical at the entrance point. They will then curve until nearly horizontal, the water then leaving striking the moving blades. The curvature of these need not be reflex, but merely turned off so as to eject the water with only axial velocity. The curvature of both guides and vanes is, of course, at right angles to the plane of the wheel ; *not* in the same plane, as is the case with the two other types.

Having now pointed out the principles of *form* in the wheel, we must discuss the size.

D

It is to be here noticed that the turbine is more particularly suited for high falls. The "reaction" class is used when there is a good supply of water, and the "impulse" when this is more limited.

In the *reaction* type (which is most used and is generally referred to in above descriptions) the first point to be settled is the quantity of water passing, as determined by measurements of the stream. Next, the radial velocity. A practical rule much used is that this shall be one-eighth that which would arise merely from the head of water, and this equals $\frac{1}{8}$ × 8·06 × square root of head in feet; or, more roughly, radial velocity in feet per second = square root of head in feet. Knowing this, and the quantity flowing, we have—

Area of water passage in square feet.

$$= \frac{\text{quantity in cubic feet per second}}{\text{velocity feet per second}}.$$

This area must be provided in the following places:—

1. Everywhere in the pipes leading to and from the turbine.

2. In the guide chamber.

3. In the total surface area of the guide openings taken at right angles to the direction of flow.

4. In the total area of the vane openings both inside and outside the revolving portion of the turbine.

It is customary to make the inside radius of the revolving part half that of the outside, and thus neglecting the thickness of the blades (upwards of $\frac{1}{2}$ in. each), we have the breadth of the wheel at the inner circumference of the rotor to be twice that at the outer circumference. This proportion usually is adopted in the design.

The only other point to consider is the velocity of the outer circumference of the rotor, which usually is about two-thirds the velocity due to the head, *i.e.*, $\frac{2}{3}$ × 8·06 × square root of head in feet = about 5 times square root of head in feet.

The actual velocity of approach will be a little more than this, depending on the friction in the water passages.

If the entrance angle in the rotor vanes is to be other than rectangular with the leaving angles of the guides, this circumference velocity will be more or less than this value, according as the angle is directed towards or from the guides, as already explained.

If it is rectangular the work per second is found by the rule already referred to—

Momentum per second × velocity feet per second
= work in foot-pounds per second ; *i.e.*,

$$\frac{\text{Gallons of water per sec.} \times 10 \text{ lbs.} \times (\text{velocity in ft. per sec.})^2}{32}$$

= foot-pounds per second, which, divided by 550 = horse power. The efficiency of a turbine (*i.e.*, apart from that of the water passages) is upwards of 80 per cent, or including the passages about 60 per cent. It must be clearly understood, however, that this efficiency depends on the wheel being run at the speed for which it is also designed. The efficiency will be less at the other speeds, whether these speeds are lesser or greater. If the water velocity increases, the wheel will not be efficient as regards the departure of the water on the inner circumference. If too slow, the relative velocity of the wheel and water will alter, thus causing the leaving velocity to be other than radial in direction, with resulting eddies and loss by friction.

Turbines are thus not so well suited for variable water energy as water wheels, and we usually conduct the water through specially-formed channels, with sluice gates or valves to control the supply. These are frequently automatically operated by a governor. This latter may be a mechanical device, like a steam governor, driven by the turbine, or may depend for its motion on the changing position of a float.

In considering the use of the turbine for a particular purpose we find the actual energy of the water supplied reduced by the machine's efficiency as already given, and balance it against the work to be done in the power station. Thus—

Work of water in turbine × efficiency of shafting
and mechanism of transmission

= work on machinery (torque in foot-pounds × 6·28
× revolutions per second ÷ 550 = horse power).

The use of the turbine has enabled us to harness great falls of water, such as Niagara, and, by coupling it with electric generating machinery and electric mains, convey the power to a great distance.

Classifying the 'machines described up to the present, we have the following arrangement :—

Machine.	Natural or forced condition.	Purpose.
Presses and press mechanisms.	Great head.	Great forces with slow motion.
Water wheels.	Moderate head, varying velocity.	Moderate torque and velocity.
Turbines.	Great heads.	Great torques and velocities.

The turbine is thus seen to be the most wide in its application, but it cannot be too clearly pointed out that it is only very valuable when a continuous and not very greatly changing supply of water is available.

With reference to the impulse turbines, as mentioned, these are suitable for smaller supplies and greater heads. The area of the water passages will, of course, be greater than that necessitated by quantity and velocity.

CHAPTER VII.

PUMPS.

ALTHOUGH a pump is a machine intended to give energy to water, not to take energy from it, from its frequent use in hydraulic engineering it calls for detailed discussion.

There are three classes of pumps :—

1. Reciprocating.
2. Centrifugal.
3. Jet.

All depend for their action on the reduction of atmospheric pressure within a containing vessel, the outside pressure forcing water into the space. The normal pressure of the atmosphere is nearly 15 lbs. per square inch, which pressure is also equivalent to about 33 ft. head of water (or 30 in. of mercury). If, then, we can produce a good vacuum in the container, water will rise upwards of 33 ft. under the air pressure. In practice we can rarely exceed 25 ft. or 26 ft. lift, this corresponding to the highest vacuum which ordinary mechanism can produce.

In the *reciprocating* type we have a moving piston in a cylinder, the rear (or lower end) of which is accessible to the supply water by means of a suction pipe, the admission being through an inward-opening valve. As the piston advances the space left (which at first contains air) increases and the air expanding decreases pressure. The pressure on the supply water, remaining constant (arising from the external atmosphere), pushes the water in the suction pipe towards the cylinder, and if the reduction of pressure is sufficient, and the height of the pipe not more than 26 ft., some will enter by the cylinder. On the return stroke of the piston the air and water in the rear end of the cylinder is compressed, shutting the beforementioned valve, and forcing the fluid through an outward-opening valve in the piston or cylinder wall. This valve was previously kept shut by the greater air and water pressure on the outside.

We have thus a certain quantity of water drawn into the cylinder on the forward stroke and pushed out on the

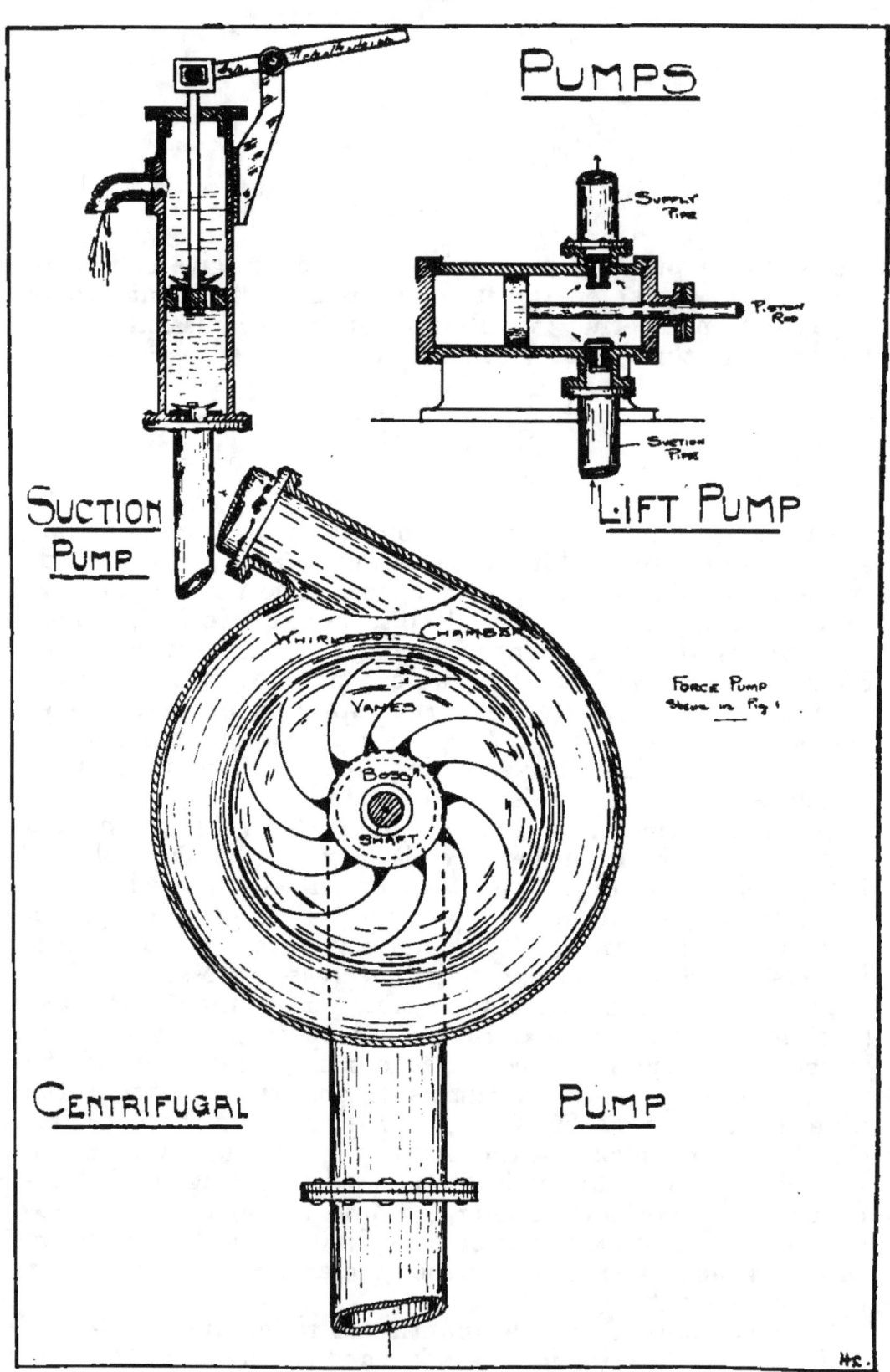

PUMPS

SUCTION PUMP

LIFT PUMP

SUPPLY PIPE

PISTON ROD

SUCTION PIPE

WHIRLPOOL CHAMBER

VANES

BOSS

SHAFT

FORCE PUMP
Shown in Fig. 1.

CENTRIFUGAL PUMP

FIG. 18.

return. As soon as all the air has gone, the discharge per stroke will be the full capacity of the space left in the cylinder by the piston.

Hence we have—

Area in square feet of cylinder × single stroke in feet

× number of double strokes per second

= quantity pumped in cubic feet per second.

This multiplied by the height to which it is raised, and by $62\frac{1}{2}$ to convert to pounds, gives the work done in foot-pounds, thus :—

$$\frac{\text{Area of cylinder} \times \text{stroke} \times \text{number of double strokes} \times \text{height in feet} \times 62\frac{1}{2}}{550} = \text{H.P.}$$

It is customary to discriminate between three classes of reciprocating pump by the following names :—

1. Suction.
2. Lift.
3. Force.

These do not differ at all in principle, but merely in the arrangement of the valves.

The *suction* pump has the outward-opening valve in the centre of the piston or plunger, the rod which drives it being forked so as to give space for same. On the up or working stroke the water above the piston is lifted on it to a pipe which removes it by gravitation.

The *lift* pump is identical with the suction pump, but has, in addition, another outward-opening valve in the upper part of the cylinder in another container, so that water is retained when lifted, and raised higher by the next stroke's supply of water.

The additional height to which the water is raised must, of course, be considered in the work done.

The *force* pump is the most useful, and has the outward-opening valve in the cylinder barrel, so that on the return stroke the water is forced out into another container, and by continuous working can be lifted to any height above the pump up to the limit of the work put in and the strength of the parts.

It is usual to have pumps for hydraulic purposes double-acting, *i.e.*, pumping and forcing on both strokes. The illustration in fig. 1 shows a Worthington double-acting force pump, in which it will be noticed that there are valves on both sides of the piston, so that while one side is forcing up water the other side is being filled by the atmospherically-pressed water. The work of such a pump as this is, of course, double that of the single-acting pump, and the supply of water is more continuous.

In order to render the flow fairly free from the pulsation which necessarily occurs as the result of the reciprocating

Fig. 19.—Belt-driven Pump.

motion of the pump, the supply pipe usually enters a cylindrical vessel containing air. By its pressure it compresses the air, and when this pressure is slightly relieved at the end of each stroke of the pump the expansion of the air drives the water out with a less rapidly varying velocity than would occur if there were no air vessel. This vessel will be noticed above the Worthington pump.

In designing a pump we have first to discover at what depth the water is, and put our pump not more than 26 ft. above its permanent level. In deep shafts, such as occur in mines, and also where the water is situated at a great depth, the pump is frequently driven by an engine on or near the surface of the ground with rods, working between roller guides, conveying power to the pumps.

Next we have to consider the capacity of the pump, having regard to the quantity to be pumped. It must be noted that the water has to pass through the following places: (1) The suction pipe; (2) the entrance valves; (3) the cylinder; (4) the exit valves; (5) the supply pipe.

All these must be of sufficient area, having regard to the velocity of flow, to pass the required quantity of water per second. We shall be tied by the cylinder measurements and the piston velocity. If the mean velocity of the piston is, say, 300 ft. per minute, *i.e.*, 5 ft. per second, and the cross-sectional area of the cylinder is 2 square feet, then the utmost quantity available is 10 cubic feet per minute in a double-acting pump, or 5 ft. per minute in a single-acting one, and this quantity, taken through the whole system, will give the areas and velocities, the product of which, at any section of the water passage, necessarily equalling the quantity.

Having determined the quantity, we must find the power to be supplied by the rule—

Weight per second × total height in feet
= work in foot-pounds per second.

This multiplied by

$$\frac{1}{\text{efficiency of pump}}$$

will give the effective horse power which is to be supplied by the steam engine or other prime mover.

The efficiency of a good pump is upwards of 75 per cent, and so four-thirds of the work to be done will give the work to be supplied by the engine. (Note that there is here no account taken of the steam-engine efficiency, which has also to be considered.)

The *centrifugal* pump very much resembles a turbine in its construction, but, of course, the flow of the water is reversed. The suction pipe is usually forked, and the water is led to the centre of the wheel on each side. There are no fixed guides, and the water, after passing through the vanes of a rotor, which give it energy of motion and pressure energy, circulates in a concentric vessel, called a whirlpool chamber, in which its energy of motion alters to pressure energy, in addition to the pressure energy which is given to it by the rotor.

The object aimed at is to convert entirely to pressure energy before leaving the pump, so that there may be no great loss by eddy friction in the supply pipe which leads tangentially from the whirlpool chamber. We have thus the following cycle of changes:—

1. Water rising in suction main by atmospheric pressure. (This is started by air being driven out of the pump by the vanes.)

2. Water entering vanes with only radial velocity acquires velocity of rotation and pressure in the rotor.

3. Water leaves the vanes with its acquired velocity of rotation, and converts this into pressure energy by circulating in whirlpool chamber.

Fig. 20.— Compound Duplex Pump.

4. Water enters the supply main with considerable pressure energy, which raises it to a reservoir, where it stores potential energy.

The best dimensions of the whirlpool chamber are somewhat uncertain, but the proportions used by makers are found to be very efficient.

The form of the vanes is determined by the following considerations:—

1. Water must enter with a radial velocity only and acquire rotary velocity in the wheel. The angle, therefore, of the vane at inner circumference (i.e., the entrance) is found by combining the velocities of radial approach and of

the vane tip by a triangle, as in the turbine, the direction of the inclined side being the direction of the vane at the tip. The vane then curves gently through the rotor to the other tip.

2. Water must leave with the maximum useful amount of kinetic energy.

This would indicate the vane tip to be radial in direction at the exit, but from practical considerations of the conversion to pressure, it is found advisable to slope back the vane so that the water leaves with a smaller velocity (about $\frac{3}{4}$) than that of the circumference of the rotor, the angle being determined by the ratio of velocities as before. From 15 deg. to 30 deg. inclination to the tangent is usual.

The work done by the pump is arrived at as in the case of the turbine.

$$\text{The momentum per sec.} = \frac{\text{weight in lbs. per sec.} \times \text{velocity in feet per sec. of water leaving rotor}}{32}$$

which again multiplied by velocity of rotor circumference gives the work done by the water. This, reduced by the efficiency of pump, usually about 60 per cent, gives the actual work done in raising the water, which, divided by the weight in pounds per second, gives the height to which the water will be raised.

The radial velocity is usually about one-quarter that which the height raised would produce in freely falling water, *i.e.*, about twice the square root of the required head in feet. The velocity of the rotor circumference is usually made eight times square root of head in feet.

The areas required through the pump will, of course, depend on the radial velocity and the quantity to be pumped. These areas must be supplied at the following places :—

1. Suction main and entrance to pump.

2. In water passage through rotor.

3. In whirlpool chamber (at right angles to direction of flow, which is rotary).

4. In supply main.

Centrifugal pumps are much more compact and easily worked than reciprocating ones, and are very portable.

Like the turbine, however, they are only most efficient when the supply is unvarying. Hence reciprocating pumps are more used for water supply and centrifugal pumps for pumping out reservoirs.

The *jet* pump is very simple, and has the enormous advantage of possessing no moving parts.

It has already been mentioned that change of velocity necessitates change of pressure, and that the balance of energy is made up in this way. If we have a very fine jet, the water issues from it with very great velocity, owing to the reduction of area ; and if this jet is placed in another main connected with a supply of water, the pressure energy being reduced to below atmospheric pressure pumping will be possible. This is an extremely useful method of pumping water when there is already a head available, and the construction is quite simple.

The hydraulic ram serves a similar purpose. Here a quantity of water falls through a certain height, and its flow is then checked by the automatic closing of a valve. The momentum acquired by the water causes sufficient force to appear at this moment to open another valve, and lift some of the water through it to a greater height than that from which it fell. As soon as the momentum the first valve re-opens and the action is repeated, a small quantity of water being raised to a great height by the energy of a larger quantity falling a lesser height.

CHAPTER VIII.

HYDRAULIC ENGINES.

IT will be noticed that the hydraulic machinery, as yet described, is either suitable to direct action with slow motion, or rotary action with rapid motion, but no medium between these extreme conditions. Gearing down the high-speed turbine will involve considerable losses by friction, besides capital expenditure, so that some other means must be sought when comparatively slow rotary motion is required. This is supplied by the water-pressure engine, which is an adaptation of the ordinary hydraulic press to a mechanism which will convert straight-line motion to circular. It is easy to understand how a reciprocating pump could be devised and used as an engine if pressure water could be continuously supplied to it at the proper times, having regard to the direction of the pressure required. Any engineer student who has given attention to heat (i.e., steam, gas, oil, and hot-air) engines will be familiar with the idea of admitting fluid to press against a piston, the motion being made reciprocating by cutting off (and in most cases reversing in the piston) the supply at proper times and places by valves. The general case of conversion of motion in this way consists of a sliding piece (to which motion is given by the piston), with a rod on a hinged joint connected to a crank on the motive shaft. When this connecting rod is in the same straight line there is no turning effect on the shaft (these positions are termed the "dead points"), and we depend for continuation of the motion on the momentum, which was previously supplied to the moving parts, or to the simultaneous action of some other connecting rod which is not in the same line as its piston rod. When the motion is slow the momentum is necessarily small, however great the pressure. It must be remembered also that great pressures necessitate large masses of metal with consequent great internal resistances.

Hence, in hydraulic engines, which are nearly always used for great torques and small angular velocities, if of single-cylinder type, we must have a very heavy fly wheel. It is, therefore, considered preferable to have two or three cylinders acting on the same shaft, with the points of attachment at 90 deg. or 120 deg. apart.

The type which is well known to steam engineers as the "Brotherhood" engine is largely used in hydraulic work. It consists of three cylinders, arranged to point towards the shaft, the angle between each centre line being 120 deg. In order to compensate for the deviation in the connecting rod, which occurs by reason of the motion of the crank, either the cylinders must be in trunnions like the old oscillating steam engine, or the connecting rod must be trunked (*i.e.*, hinged) to the piston.

It is necessary, in order to give the pistons pressure and release in the proper sequence, to use a somewhat complex arrangement of valves. If the cylinders oscillate, this motion can be used to open and cut off valves which give admission to the cylinder at the centre of oscillation (which is either at the centre or end of the cylinders) through *both* trunnions or the ends.

If the connecting rods are trunked, the valves are controlled by cams and tappets, actuated by the shaft like the petrol-engine. In order to determine the position of the valves, we have to consider the following combinations :—

1. When one piston is exerting pressure the other two must be exhausting.

2. At the moment any one piston reaches the end of its stroke the exhaust of that cylinder must be opened.

We must, therefore, have two ports admitting to the cylinder, one of which is opening when the connecting rod is moving forward and letting in pressure water. When the maximum stroke is reached, this port must be closed (either by the rotation of the cylinder or by a tappet) and immediately the exhaust valve must be opened (by the same mechanism), and the water leaves to waste as the piston returns into the cylinder.

The work of a hydraulic engine per stroke is found by taking the net pressure (*i.e.*, difference between the supply and exhaust pressures) on the piston per square inch, multiplied by the piston area × length of stroke in feet. This multiplied by number of revolutions per second ÷ 550 = horse power. (Reduce by efficiency as usual.)

It is usual to have the water supply and exhaust mutually convertible, so that the engine can be stopped on the middle position and reversed by changing the exhaust to the supply.

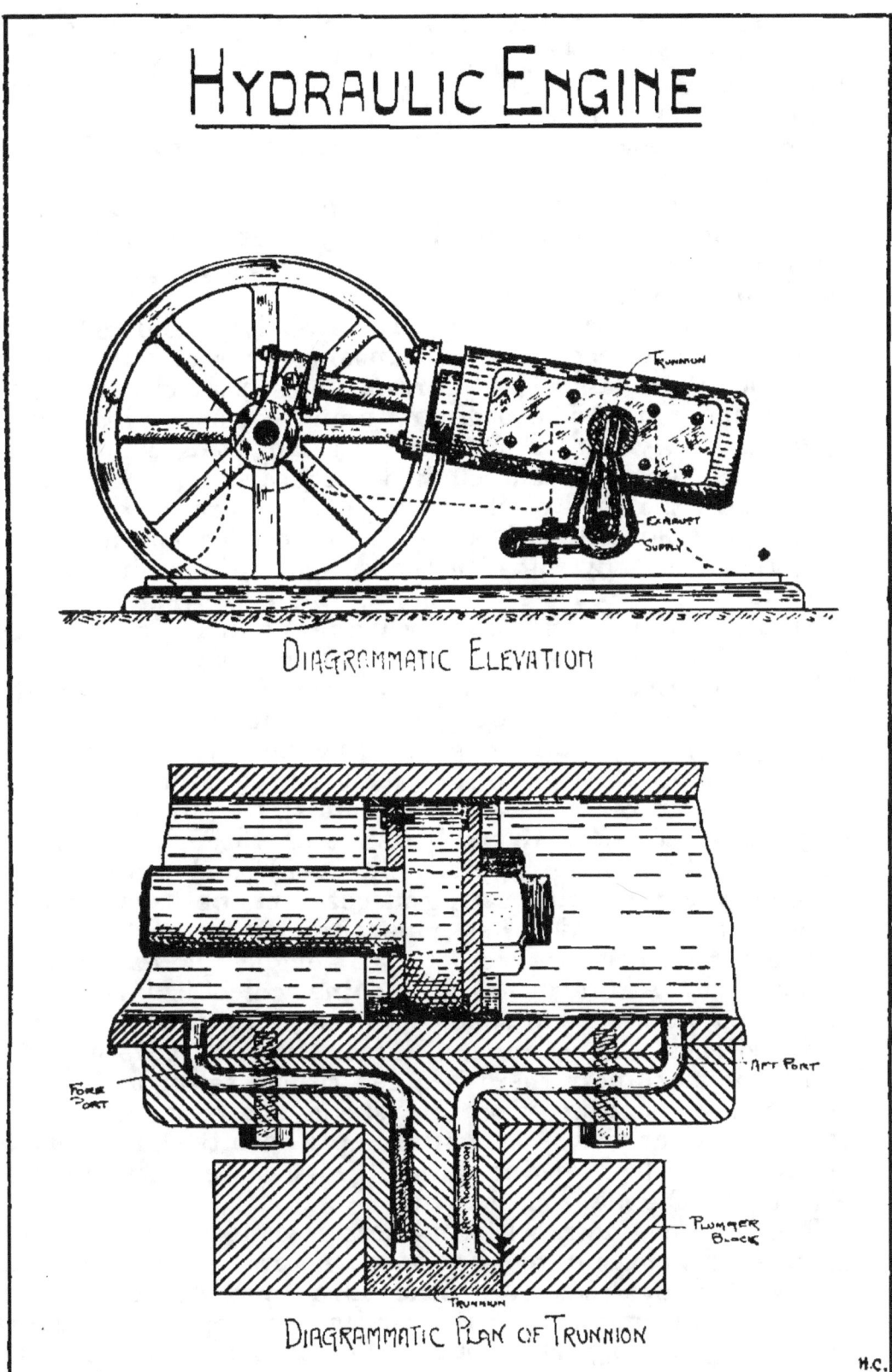

HYDRAULIC ENGINE

DIAGRAMMATIC ELEVATION

DIAGRAMMATIC PLAN OF TRUNNION

FIG. 21.

There are an enormous number of applications of the hydraulic engine. In any machine in which great forces are to be exerted, but with comparatively low velocities, the engine is applicable.

Swing bridges, capstans, tillers, gun carriages, and hoists are notable examples.

In modern warships hydraulic machinery plays a great part. The gun turrets are slewed by hydraulic engines, the steering mechanism is operated by hydraulic engines, and the loading done by hydraulic cranes.

In regard to cranes, we have already considered those which act by direct pressure transmitted by chains. There is yet another class which corresponds in its construction to the steam crane. The ordinary crane consists of a drum, which is slowly rotated by toothed gearing, this being driven by a steam engine. The chain for the drum (or "winch") passes over the head of the "jib," or long arm of the crane, and, acting through a sheave-block suspended on the chain, lifts the load. By substituting a hydraulic engine of the type just described we can obtain more conveniently very great lifting force, and cranes capable of lifting 50 and 100 tons are now quite common in dock practice.

The majority of water meters used for measuring the quantity of water passing through a conduit are now designed on the hydraulic engine principle. The quantity of water passing through will necessarily equal the capacity of the clear space in the cylinder, multiplied by the number of strokes, so that if we pass water through an engine (doing, of course, no appreciable work), and connecting a counter with the reciprocating mechanism, we have a record of the quantity which has gone through.

Another important use of the engine is in "relay" mechanism. A "relay" is a machine which is intended to act as an auxiliary to some other machine working valves and switches. Thus in the larger type of governor for hydraulic machinery there is a centrifugal set of balls, such as we are familiar with on steam engines. The levers operated by the rise of the balls simply open the supply valve of a small "relay" engine, which throttles the valve or sluice controlling the main mechanism.

Electrical engineers will doubtless recognise the similarity in this arrangement to the relay motors, which are used to work the high-tension switches in a power station.

In marine practice it is usually inconvenient to store pressure water by an accumulator of the previously described type, and we hence use an arrangement of double cylinders and pistons like the "intensifier," with steam from the ship's boilers acting on one piston, and transmitting its pressure to water on the other piston. Such an arrangement is very much more economical of space, and by proportioning the piston areas very great water pressures can be produced.

The application of the hydraulic engine to the tiller gives rise to an interesting mechanism. The engine is of the two or three cylinder type, and rotates a crank shaft upon which are keyed two other wheels gearing by bevel wheels to a horizontal toothed wheel. The latter gears with a toothed sector on the deck, so that when pressure water is admitted the engine rotates as a whole about the centre of the sector, and turns with it the tiller. The supply is led in through the central trunnion or through flexible tubing.

A similar toothed-sector mechanism is employed in raising the bascules of drawbridges, the sector being vertical and rigidly fixed to the bascule (this latter is, of course, counterbalanced behind the turning point). The Tower Bridge in London is a famous example of this arrangement.

There are numerous other cases in which these engines may be advantageously employed, such as in conveyers, turntables, etc., the important feature to be noticed being the immunity from fire risks, the facility of fixing the perfect control, and the absence of noise and vibration. Wherever a main can be taken an engine can be placed: the foundations required are much less massive than those needed for gas or steam engines, and, in the event of breakage, there is no explosion, the position is at once evident and the defect easily repaired.

•

E

CHAPTER IX.

Tidal Power.

It should be clearly understood by now that wherever there is a quantity of water possessing potential pressure or kinetic energy power can be obtained from it. In ordinary practice the sources are lakes (natural or artificial), running streams, and underground springs; but we shall sooner or later be able to utilise a far greater source of power than any of these.

Owing to the motion of the sun and moon *relatively* to any point on the earth and their attraction, there occurs twice a day at most places on the sea coast a rise and fall of the water level. This change depends on the respective positions of the sun and moon, and local conditions of current and coast line. When the sun and moon are in the same straight line (*i.e.*, new and full moon) the tides ("spring tides") have the greatest range. At the first and third quarters (*i.e.*, when the moon is half in shadow) the attractions are opposed, and the tides ("neap tides") not so great. Hence the greatest change of level we can rely on at all times is that of the neap tides, which average in this country, and in many parts of the world, about 10 feet.

The quantity of water available is quite unlimited as regards the outside supply, but it is limited by considerations of the area of the water passage through which it is admitted and the head of water outside; also by the capacity of the reservoir into which we take water during high tide.

The velocity with which the water will flow into a reservoir is determined by the heads at both ends of the communication pipe, neglecting friction

$$= 8 \times \text{square root of } net \text{ head in feet.}$$

This multiplied by the area will give the quantity which will enter through the communication channels. Having considered this, the system to be adopted is briefly the following:—

1. A conduit admitting water during the part of the flow of the tide; the difference of head inside and outside deter-

mines the velocity of flow. As the reservoir fills there will be decreasing head.

2. One, or preferably two, reservoirs filled at each tide. If two are used, one can be kept at a greater head than the other, the second being kept at constant level by a float-controlled valve, power being taken from it with a constant head as from an accumulator.

The waste from the machinery will, of course, be discharged during the ebb of the tide.

If desirable, the kinetic energy of the entering water can be used in a turbine, but this is not very convenient, as the inside head will be much reduced, and also the flow is not continuous. By making the reservoirs large enough to hold several days' supply, the head water can be used for turbines or pressure engines, the emptying tanks being replenished at intervals by sluices between the two tanks, the first being refilled when shut off from the second.

We have, therefore, in designing a tidal plant, to consider the following conditions :—

1. The level of work must not be below but near to the low-tide mark, power being transferred to higher levels by transmission mechanism.

2. The energy storage of the reservoirs must be in excess of the amount of work required of them during the interval between successive fillings, preferably two or three times.

Thus, if we require 100 horse power continuously, and the tanks are filled every 12 hours, we must at least have $100 \times 33,000 \times 60 \times 12 = 2,376,000,000$ foot-pounds of work available, allowing for losses and storage, say, 5,000,000,000. Taking the mean available head at 5 ft., this means one thousand million pounds of water must be stored every day and free passage given to it through all water passages. This means nearly $1\frac{1}{2}$ million pounds per minute, or about four thousand cubic feet per second, to convey which very many pipes will be necessary, and there must be a machine for each.

This indicates the crucial difficulty of tidal power, and shows that for large powers simple reservoirs are almost impracticable.

Water wheels for small powers can, of course, be quite easily worked by the flow of water between sea and reservoir, and *vice versâ*, the return flow acting upon the wheel in the same way as a flow by a change of the sluices.

Similarly we may increase the working pressure, which will normally be only that corresponding to the head of water in the reservoirs, by admitting water from the bottom into an intensifier, which multiplies the pressure. On the back stroke water can be admitted into the high-pressure cylinder by an inward-opening valve. This arrangement is one of the most practical that has been devised.

Another very important feature in connection with tidal power is economy. The first cost of cutting large reservoirs and putting down conduits, etc., will involve a large expenditure of capital, which, if it produces a money value in power per annum which happens to be less than that which could be obtained from prime movers in the same time at a cost of the recognised earning value of the said capital, then the latter is not put out to any advantage. From the few figures given it will be seen that, proportionately to the space occupied by the works, the power is very small, owing to the narrow range of head. We cannot go below the normal ebb-tide level, because the water has to be returned, nor can we get per pound of water more than the height of the tide head in feet.

The economical features are, then, very important, and at the present, except for very small powers and with naturally convenient formation of the land, the use of this source of energy is almost prohibited from this cause.

There can be little doubt, however, that in the comparatively near future, especially when coal, which is at present almost the entire source of energy for power purposes, becomes more scarce, the tides will be employed, especially in those places where, owing to the formation of the coast, there is a big range in feet, and the problem should be well studied by the young engineer.

Tidal rivers are rather more promising, as there is a continuous fall in the river, and also there is an additional velocity head from the flow. A river dammed serves the same purpose as a lake, the water being released through machinery, which will utilise its stored head.

Disadvantages also appear in this connection, however, especially in rivers where there are towns on the banks. It is a fairly well established fact that the continuous flow of rivers is largely essential to their purity. so that the conversion of a river into a lake would, in the presence of a great city, possibly prove a source of danger to health.

Furthermore, when the soil is, as usually occurs, porous, there will be a permanent increase in the level of the ground water, with resultant insanitary conditions and deterioration of property. The first cost of damming a wide and swift river is also very great, and there will be certain expenses involved in the upkeep and control of the sluices.

Waterfalls are the most satisfactory source of power, as we have in these the great essential of head. The famous falls of Niagara, in America, have been utilised to produce many thousands of horse power by the construction of tapping canals, drop shafts, and turbines, the supply being converted into electrical energy and transmitted to distant towns by cables.

The economical factor here diminishes in proportion to the output of power, so that although very great capital expenditure is involved, there is a speedy return; and there can be no doubt that all the great falls in the world will be used in this way sooner or later.

The question of the "load factor," or proportion between the average and maximum power to be given out at the source of energy, has a very material effect on the question of installing machinery. Although the plant may be running for some few hours at a great profit, during the rest of the day there often is little or no call for its work, and during that time the cost of wear and tear, salaries, and rents still must be paid, and in the case of some hydraulic machinery which cannot be stopped, there will be actual waste of power. This may, however, be frequently stored in chemical accumulators ("secondary cells").

CHAPTER X.

WATER SUPPLY.

ONE of the most important branches of hydraulic engineering is the supply of water for drinking and sanitary purposes. The natural sources of supply are usually springs situated at some depth. These springs arise from the accumulation of rain water, which, percolating through the soil, has finally rested on an impervious stratum. The shafts sunk to the springs are termed wells, and are of three types:—

1. Shallow.
2. Deep.
3. Artesian.

The shallow well is one which is sunk through the surface soil to near the surface of an impervious stratum. Water which has accumulated at the lowest level on this stratum is obtainable in this way, but unless situated at a considerable depth the water is very likely to have become contaminated by vegetation and, in towns, sewage from the soil.

Deep wells are those which pass through one impervious stratum to another and tap the water lying on the lower. By filtration through the soil it will generally have been much purified, but is, of course, liable to contain mineral matter.

Artesian wells are those which tap supplies that are stored in the basin-like formations which occur in many parts of the world. There is in these cases a great dip extending through many strata, causing eventually a large quantity of water to be stored, which has everywhere an available head corresponding to the lowest point of outlet from the basin. When wells are driven right down to the pervious materials between the impervious strata where the water has accumulated, the pressure drives it up the shaft to the same level as its highest point. This may or may not be above the ground level at the point where the shaft is sunk, according to the levels attained by the lower of the impervious strata and the local conditions controlling the flow of the water.

If the water is supplied above ground level, as often occurs in the artesian type, then no pumping is required, and the system is said to be a *gravitational* one.

More frequently pumping is necessary, and reciprocating pumps are usually employed. In the older methods, beam-engines and vertically-acting force pumps were used ; but the horizontal double-acting type, like the Worthington, is more and more used where possible, particularly on account of the small losses of transmission, the steam-engine piston and pump plunger being on the same rod. After pumping, it passes through conduits to an impounding reservoir, where are kept upwards of 300 days' supply of water. (This is computed on the demand, 20 gallons upwards per head per day being the usual requirement). It then is transferred through sand filters (the water must pass upwards or downwards through the entire thickness of these) to supply reservoirs for immediate use. These are covered in to keep out the light, which encourages the growth of organisms, and to exclude dust from the atmosphere. Upwards of ten days' supply is kept in the reservoirs, and drawn upon from there as required. The cross-sectional areas of the mains are determined by the velocity which the head in the reservoir produces, considered together with the quantity to be supplied (including emergency provision for fire).

The following well-known rule, based on the friction of surface rubbing, enables us to calculate the head required in the pipe (*i.e.*, the total fall) to maintain the velocity :—

Velocity feet per second = 50 × square root of

$$\left[\frac{(\text{diameter of pipe in feet}) \times (\text{fall in feet})}{\text{length in feet} + 50 \text{ diameters in feet}} \right]$$

whence head or fall in feet of pipe

$$= \frac{(\text{velocity in ft. per sec.})^2 \times (\text{length in ft.} + 50 \text{ diameters})}{2500 \text{ diameters}}$$

(This is known as " Eytelwein's formula.")

At various points where this fall brings the pipes to low levels pumping stations have to be put down, which can continuously pump a rather larger quantity than the pipes deliver to a level from which pipes can again fall, so that the whole of the area to be served is covered.

The water mains diminish in size down to 12 in. or even 6 in. cast-iron pipes, about 6 ft. long, with socketed joints, caulked with lead. Iron unions are screwed into these, or, preferably, into specially-made joints, and heavy lead pipes (drawn by hydraulic pressure already described) are screwed to them by a back nut, and then taken to the house. These lead pipes, termed the rising mains, are led to a cistern at the highest level in the house to which the water pressure will lift the supply, and from there smaller pipes run to the various taps, cocks being inserted at various points to control the supply. The house supplies are either intermittent, where there is a large cistern filled each day, or continuous, where a smaller cistern is kept at a constant level with a ball-cock valve, which cuts off the supply when that level is obtained.

Fire, street-watering, and sewer-flushing hydrants are simply large taps with screw-down valves connected with the street mains. There is a hose "union," or connection to which the flushing hose is screwed, fitted to each. The hose consists of 60 ft. lengths of riveted leather or wire-bound india-rubber tubing with gun-metal "unions," and a nozzle fitted with a cock. Hose needs constant attention, as the nature of the materials used is such as to rapidly deteriorate with use.

Hot-water supply in houses is arranged by conveying into the bottom of a boiler a pipe from the cold-water supply or "feed tank," an exit pipe from the top of the boiler removing it by its expansion as it warms. From the same cause it ascends the pipe to the taps. The pipe is continued past the taps and descends again to the boiler, entering at the bottom. (Frequently it is simply connected to the cold-water feed pipe.) We thus have a circuit (termed "flow and return ") maintained by the rise of the hot water and sinking of the cold, on account of the greater weight of the latter. In most cases the circuit is arranged in duplicate, so as to get more rapid heating, one or more auxiliary hot-water cylinders or tanks being placed in the system.

Water which contains a large amount of chalk in solution is said to be "hard," and is then unsuitable for cleansing purposes. Up to a certain small limit it is not injurious to drink. The water dissolves much more chalk when it also contains carbonic acid gas, and consequently, when the water is boiled, the gas being driven off, some of the chalk precipitates and crusts boilers and hot-water pipes. From the same cause the supply mains gradually become incrusted, and have to be scraped out periodically. Hard water does not so readily act upon metals and other substances, so that it is advantageous when lead pipes are used.

In regard to cisterns, these are usually made of galvanised iron plates, $\frac{1}{8}$ in. upwards in thickness, connected together with angle irons and rivets.

Cylinders and cylindric boilers may be calculated for strength by the following rule (side pressure is considered, as the cylinder is weakest that way):—

$$\text{Thickness of metal (inches)} = \frac{\text{pressure lbs. per sq. in.} \times \text{diameter in ins.}}{2 \times 5 \text{ tons per inch} \times 2240}$$

The thick pipes which are required for the water mains will be calculated by the rule already given for hydraulic mains. The following points must be considered in arriving at a right estimate of the relation between the head available at the source of supply and at the house:—

1. Loss of head by friction through main sluices when leaving supply reservoirs.

2. Loss of head by rubbing in the main supply pipe, together with losses at changes of section and curvature in that pipe.

3. Loss of head in branch pipe due to change of section from main pipe.

4. Rubbing friction in branch pipe.

5. Friction at all valves and connections.

We should have finally, at the moment of entering the house, sufficient head to raise it up to the level of the cistern (preferably in the roof).

It is very convenient to make a diagram (like that in fig. 2) showing the loss of energy or "head" in feet per pound of water through the whole system.

In this way we can at once tell what is the efficiency at any point, and what pressure will be available if we take a pipe at or below the level of this "hydraulic gradient."

In connection with the friction of the pipes, the question of incrustation also arises. In pipes which have been laid some time the effective diameter is very greatly reduced, and the co-efficient of friction also increases from the irregularity of the section, and also to some extent from the nature of the surface of the pipe, which has changed from smooth metal to a rough crust.

The hydraulic gradient is also very useful in determining how much we may, when we wish, deviate from the continuous down grade of the mains. For crossing valleys and rivers it is frequently necessary to put in a dip or "anti-syphon" to avoid forming an aqueduct. So long as no part of the pipe is above the level of hydraulic gradient (necessarily drawn in feet of height or "head" above a datum line) flow will be maintained, although, of course, energy will be absorbed in ascending the up-grade of pipe, so that the pressure will fall considerably. At any point in the pipe which may come above the hydraulic gradient, there will tend to form a partial vacuum. This will usually be filled with air previously dissolved in water, so that the syphonic tendency will be very small.

CHAPTER XI.

Sewage Carriage and Disposal.

The arrangement of a sewage disposal system is almost exactly the reverse of water supply, and may well be compared to the system of veins in the human body, which remove the impure blood brought by the arteries. In water supply, we commence at the reservoir and end with the house. In sewage, we always commence with the house and end with the sewage tank. In some parts, a dry system of dealing with sewage is still used, but its insanitariness and inconvenience is now clearly recognised ; and all modern engineers are agreed as to the superiority of the water-carriage system.

Sewage consists of organic excreta, solid and liquid, sink and bath water, and in the combined system rain water is also mixed with it. The "separate system" provides for organic refuse only, rain water being conveyed away by a separate system of pipes. By some this arrangement is considered superior, but its first cost is greater, and sewers are not so self-cleansing as those of the combined system, in which there is a far greater quantity of liquid matter. Sewage on exposure and in the presence of water undergoes decomposition, producing very unpleasant odour and appearance. It is also very good medium for the cultivation of bacteria, so that disease germs, if present, are likely to be disseminated. The ideal system is one which will remove the material before decomposition commences to a place where it may be dealt with in one of the following ways :—

1. *Discharged into the sea or mouth of a river* at ebb tide, so that it may be broken up and gradually converted to harmless compounds by the action of sea water and the gases and organisms it contains.

This, of course, is not at all satisfactory in the proximity of a city, or if the sea within any comparatively small distance is the source of any food supply.

2. *Used for Manuring Purposes.*—Decomposition occurs here under natural limitations of position, and the material

breaks up into harmless organic substances, which are very suitable for fertilising soil. From this use for sewage has originated the word " sewage farm."

3. *Chemically Treated.*—The main sewers are led into a series of tanks adding one of the following chemicals to the sewage :—

(*a*) Ferrozone (" International " process) ;

(*b*) Alumino-ferric ;

(*c*) Lime, with or without salts of alumina or iron magnetite,

Which cause " precipitation" (*i.e.*, a chemical change with the separating out of solids, which fall to the bottom). Result, " sludge," which is used for manure. The liquid " effluent " is then filtered downwards through beds and discharged into a stream nearly pure.

Automatic tanks are usually employed in the sewers, which fill slowly and empty rapidly by syphonic action.

(4) *Bacterially Treated* (" Septic " process).—It is now known that decomposition occurs by the agency of certain very very minute vegetable organisms known as microbes or bacteria. By making conditions suited to the growth of these we can facilitate the decomposition to such an extent that a very little time is occupied before the sewage can be turned out as harmless.

We first turn the liquid sewage into a covered septic tank and let it stand for some hours. During this time bacteria termed " anaërobes " develop and break up the sewage into exceedingly small parts.

It will be understood that the friction in the sewers has already broken up the solid matter to a very great extent.

The material is now admitted through pipes running under a series of " bacteria beds," through which it passes upwards, emerging on the surface, and finally escaping by an overflow to some stream.

These " bacteria beds " are similar to filter beds in water-works, but the pieces of stone are rather larger, and, instead of endeavouring to get the bed full of liquid, our object should be to merely get each piece of stone (any hard durable material is suitable) covered with a film of liquid. Under these circumstances " aërobes " develop and destroy all organic life in the sewage, so that when it leaves the bed (in which it is allowed to remain for about 12 hours or so) it is free from all dangerous impurities. To keep the even distribution, special sprinklers, sometimes rotary, are often employed instead of upward filtration.

Each of the systems described has advantages when regarded from all points of view.

Elaborate chemical and septic processes are very difficult and costly for large cities, but are eminently suitable for small works. Direct discharge or partial chemical treatment, therefore, have favour in large installations, but cannot be regarded as finally satisfactory.

It is usually necessary to pump the sewage one or more times before treatment, owing to the continuous fall of the mains. It very rarely happens that the land is so inclined as to avoid pumping, even when large sewers with very little fall are employed, but very frequently it is only necessary to pump once, and this is done at the sewage farm, so that most of the smaller installations consist of a pumping station and sewage tanks situated near some river or sea front.

Tracing the sewage from the house to the works we have the following series : Within the house, water closets, urinals, sinks, baths, and surface-water gullies taking rain from roof and yards. Those pipes which take the sewage proper are termed soil pipes, and above the ground are of heavy drawn or cast lead. They are connected with soldered joints to each and every fitting by branch pipes, and usually left open above the roof-level for ventilation. A bend is made either in the fitting or in the pipe near to it, so that by the accumulation of water in this bend or " trap " gases are shut out of the house.

Water closets and urinals are provided with flushing tanks for cleaning and emptying them, the water also serving the purpose of diluting and breaking up the sewage.

The lead soil pipe is connected to an underground stoneware or cast-iron drain, the connection being made direct with a brass " thimble," a length of tube which is soldered to the lead and cemented to the drain. Rain-water pipes are usually of cast iron, and discharge over earthenware gullies, which trap off sewer gas, and are connected with stoneware branch pipes to the main drains.

The main drain passes from its highest level through one or more access chambers, the last of which cuts off gas connection between the house and the sewer by a " trap " in the pipe.

Into the chamber air is admitted from an inward-opening ventilator, so that the house system may be kept pure by the circulation through it of air rising by expansion. This part of the system does not, as a rule, work very satisfactorily.

Passing from the intercepting "chamber" to the main sewer, usually with a quick fall, we pass from a 4 in. or 6 in. stoneware pipe into a 12 in. one, or a brick sewer of circular or egg-shaped section, from 18 in. upwards in size. This continues gradually increasing in size and decreasing in fall, with access chamber at every important junction, and change of direction until we come to the "outfall" at the sewage works.

There are usually in the course of a large sewer two or more "penstocks" or sluices, by shutting down which and releasing we can flush the sewer, but it is usually necessary to also flush with additional water.

The sewers, particularly the brick ones, tend to silt up with deposit and have to be continually cleaned out, particularly when the falls and consequently the velocities are small.

In small country services the sewage is frequently conveyed by similar means to a specially-constructed well or cesspool, made water tight with concrete and clay, the sewage being removed at intervals by a chain pump, and used as manure.

About 20 gallons of sewage per head per day is the usual allowance, so that the quantity to be treated in densely-populated districts is enormous; and when we have a combined system, and there occurs a heavy rainfall, the call upon the pumps is very great at the sewage works. It is usual to have near the outfall of a sewer storm sewers, with which communication is made over a sill when a certain level is reached; the water which goes through this to the stream without treatment is nearly pure.

There are several principles to be observed in the laying of pipes for conveying both water and sewage which should be clearly appreciated by the engineer:—

1. As far as possible pipes should communicate direct from point to point and at a uniform gradient ("slope").

2. At all changes of section, level, and direction, and also at intervals in unchanging lengths, we must have access chambers or manholes sunk from the surface, so that obstacles may be removed and the pipes cleared.

3. The pipes should preferably always run full bore, so as

to be self-cleaning. For this reason smaller stoneware drains are replacing the large brick drains in branch sewers.

4. All connections should be run into the main, of which they are tributaries, at a point of convenient access, usually a manhole.

5. The invert (*i.e.*, the lower surface) of the pipes should be continuous. It is not so essential that the top line also should be continuous, but it is certainly desirable. especially in the smaller bore pipes.

6. All connections between branch and main drains must be trapped, so that gas is prevented from passing into the branch drains.

7. Each length of sewer should be ventilated right through by inward-opening ventilators at low levels and vent pipes carried up to high levels.

8. The gradients should not vary greatly. but change continuously. At points where considerable fall is required, a chamber should be constructed to effect the fall in one sudden drop, rather than use a rapid gradient.

CHAPTER XII.

DAMS, AND SOME NOTES ON FUTURE PROSPECTS.

A RESERVOIR for power purposes is usually partly of natural formation and partly artificial. It may be necessary in some cases to build a wall right round a certain area to retain water, but more frequently a valley is chosen, which can be walled across at one or both ends. Such a wall is termed a dam.

In designing a dam, such as is shown in fig. 22, we have to consider what forces act upon it, and what their effect is upon the structure. The forces to be considered are two:—

1. The lateral pressure produced by the water.
2. The weight of the wall itself.

We have several conditions of balance to observe.

First.—The turning effect of the water upon the wall must be considerably exceeded by the resisting turning effect caused by the weight of the wall itself. It is usually considered that if the weight of the wall, multiplied by the horizontal distance of its centre of gravity from the outer third of the thickness of the base, equals the turning effect of the water about the same point that the wall is satisfactorily stable.

If the force which results from the combination of the wall's weight and the water pressure passes through this point (the division between the first and second thirds of the base from the outside), then this balance does exist. If the force passes within the point, then the wall is even more stable; if without, then it is less stable, and according as it passes on one side or other of the centre of the base, so that side will be in compression and the other side in tension. (It must be remembered that the latter is an undesirable condition for masonry, so that it must be minimised as much as possible, and should be exceeded by the direct compression caused by the downward action of the combined force now to be referred to.)

Second.—The combined force acting on any horizontal section through the wall will, in accordance with its vertical magnitude (a "component"), produce a direct compression all over that section, which will be added to the compression already produced by the turning effect and be opposed to the tension so produced.

It is very desirable that it should more than exceed the tension, so that the net result is compression. As regards the part which is in double compression, the total should not, of course, reach a "crushing" value, bearing in mind the fact that the compression produced by bending increases from zero at the centre of the section to a maximum at the edge.

Third.—The combined force on any horizontal section will also have a horizontal magnitude or "component," which in the case of dams will be rather great, and this tends to make the upper part of the wall (*i.e.*, that above the section) slide over the lower (that below the section) at every part of the wall, and more particularly towards the bottom when the pressures are great. This effect is termed shearing, and is only resisted in the wall by the mortar and friction caused by the weight of wall. Many walls, although strong enough to resist the forces caused by turning effect and weight, have failed through inability to resist this sliding effect. Hence all the mortar should be of high tensile strength, and the blocks vertically "joggled" (*i.e.*, notched one to another).

On account of the increase of pressure with the depth we increase the thickness similarly, so that the combined force is kept everywhere within the wall (the direction through the wall taken by this force is called the "line of resistance"). Hence the peculiar shape of the dam shown in the illustration. Similarly, in order to increase the resistance to turning effect (technically known as the "moment of resistance"), we frequently build a massive parapet and occasionally buttresses, so that the weight of the wall is thereby increased, throwing back the line of resistance.

In order to still further achieve this result, the inside profile is sloped back. As water pressure always acts at right angles to the surface immersed, the lower pressures will necessarily be inclined downwards, and the combined force will also partake of this inclination. The sliding tendency is also decreased by this form, but the compression is increased.

To calculate the various forces, it is necessary to consider the following important rules regarding water pressure and mechanical force :—

F

1. Pressure increases with depth of water, and at **any** point equals per square foot 62·5 × height in feet.

2. Turning effects are measured (foot-pounds) by the product of the forces (pounds) and their least distance from **the** turning point (feet)—*i.e.*, the distance at right angles from the line of direction of the force.

3. If water approaching the dam has a velocity of v feet per second the force exerted

$$= \frac{\text{weight in lbs. per second}}{32} \times v.$$

This must be added to the pressure produced by weight of water, and may be considered to act at half the height and produce the same result of turning. This total force is called the "resultant," and the point in the case of water is called the "centre of pressure."

If we draw against the side of the dam figures representing the direction and magnitude of the pressures there, as shown by dotted lines in fig. 22, then the centre of gravity of those figures will indicate the *centres of pressures on the corresponding* length of wall, as shown by the position of the large arrows, which represent resultant forces for certain layers of water.

4. Forces can be combined by the "parallelogram" (or more properly, the "triangle") of forces. [Space forbids a description of this elementary mechanical principle, but any book on mechanics describes it fully.]

Having reminded ourselves of these principles, we can apply them in the manner shown in diagram :—

First.—Divide wall and water up into horizontal layers, such that the sections of wall are approximately straight-sided.

Find the centre of gravity of each section, and also the weight of one foot run of each section of the wall, which will be the *vertical* force acting at that centre of gravity.

Second.—Find the pressures of the water at top and bottom of each layer from the height, and draw figures by setting up these pressures at the corresponding points on the wall *at right angles to the surface.*

Third.—Find the area of these figures (pounds and feet)

and their centres of gravity. The areas are equivalent to the forces in pounds acting from each layer of water, and their directions will be at right angles to surface of wall (*i.e.*, parallel to the sides of their own particular figures).

Fourth.—Produce the directions of each force, commencing at the top with the weight of the first section, and combine each with the next at the meeting points right down the wall until all the forces are combined.

Thus we shall have the following combinations :—

(*a*) Combination (by parallelogram in all cases) of weight of first section of wall with water pressure of corresponding layer.

(*b*) Resultant of (*a*) combines with weight of second section of wall.

(*c*) Resultant of (*b*) combines with water pressure from second layer.

(*d*) Resultant of (*c*) combines with weight of third section of wall, and so on.

We have thus a line running continuously down the wall of increasing force value, and increasing in outward inclination (the " line of resistance "). ·

By taking *any* horizontal section through the wall we find the following facts :—

1. The magnitude of the force in the section (*i.e.*, the value of the particular resultant where it forms part of the line).

2. The direction of that force shown by the inclination of the line.

3. The position of the combined force, *i.e.*, the point at which we can assume the whole force on the section to act shown by the intersection of the line and the plane of section.

To find the maximum tension and compression, we first multiply the force in pounds by the distance from its line of direction at 90 deg. to the centre of the section. Then , maximum tension or compression (at edge of section) in pounds per *square foot*

$$= \frac{6 \times \text{force (lbs.)} \times \text{distance (feet.)}}{(\text{width of section in feet})^2}$$

Remember that this is the turning part of the business only.

To find the direct pressure and the sliding, we split the force into horizontal and vertical components by a right-angled triangle (see diagram again). The vertical part divided by the width of the section in feet (remember we are considering one foot run of the wall) = compression in pounds per square foot.

Add this to the compression from turning and you have the maximum total compression in the section.

Subtract the tension above from this compression and you have the minimum compression in the section.

The horizontal component of the force divided by the width of the section in feet = sliding or shearing forces in pounds per square foot.

We now have the maximum and minimum compression and shearing, and from this we can easily find whether at a particular depth a certain material thickness will be satisfactory.

The strength of masonry in pounds per square foot is found in the following way :—

$$\frac{\text{crushing force (lbs. per sq. foot)}}{10 \text{ (a factor for safety)}} = \text{compression stress allowable per sq. foot (lbs.)}$$

Similarly with shearing, the actual breaking forces being found by a testing machine.

It should be particularly noticed that if the maximum tensile stress produced by turning exceeds the compression stress produced by direct action there will be tension on the edge of the section (usually the inner edge), and, if unavoidable, the jointing must be very thorough.

In the first determination of the base thickness of a dam, the following rule can be used with safety :—

$$\text{Thickness of base (feet)} = \tfrac{1}{2} \text{ height of water in feet} \times \text{square root of} \left(\frac{62 \cdot 5}{\text{weight of material in lbs. per cub. ft.}} \right)$$

This rule depends on balance being made at the outer third as already described, the inside being vertical and the outside sloped back to nothing at the top, which, although not a form actually employed, is nearly of the same efficiency as the actual form, and so may be used on account of the simplicity of the calculation.

Having thus determined the width of the base, we may adopt a form similar to that illustrated, and test it throughout by the methods detailed above.

Dams built to retain flowing water must, of course, absorb the momentum of that water, so that a great additional horizontal force will appear which will increase the turning effect, and also the sliding effect. By prolonging the outer edge of the base (the " toe "), we are able to keep the combined force within the masonry. A noteworthy example of this construction is the famous dam across the Nile at Aswân (Assouan).

In cases where stone is difficult to get, and the area available not limited, we frequently construct earth slopes on both sides of the dam, and fill in the centre with a wall of puddled (i.e., softened and rammed) clay. In Indian river practice this is frequently done, masonry being sometimes substituted for the clay. Retaining walls which will be exposed to rough seas are sloped, or, preferably, curved towards the waves, so that they are thrown back and not directly stopped.

In cases where we have water pressure continually on one side and earth pressure on the other, the turning effect on the wall may be reduced, although it must be remembered that the most adverse conditions have to be considered, such as happen when the reservoir is empty, or the earth is to be removed. In this connection it is most important to note that the walls which enclose a reservoir and at the same time retain earth should be absolutely water tight, and sufficiently massive to resist water pressure on the earth side, as, when the reservoir is empty, if water has worked behind the masonry it may strip off all the work.

Although the subject of retaining walls for earth does not properly come within a hydraulic engineer's work, yet, in those walls retaining earth and water, it is important to be able to compare the pressures.

The earth retained tends to produce lateral pressure just as water, but to a less degree, depending on the density and compactness of the material. Thus very soft clays and sands must be regarded as fluids, whereas hard rock may not need to be retained at all. A measure of this durability is found in the angle to which the material slopes back when exposed to the weather. For firm clays and other comparatively soft materials this angle is about half a right angle, and in this case the pressure is about one-fifth that which occurs with water at the same level.

The stability of the wall may be enhanced by constructing steps in the earth side of the wall, or by putting internal buttresses (counterforts) or external buttresses, increasing the weight and leverage of the mass.

In the case of reservoirs which have to be covered, the most usual manner of constructing them is to erect at intervals of 10 ft. or so square brick piers or cast-iron columns, between which are thrown brick arches forming a system of barrel vaulting. Above this, we level up with concrete to an even surface.

The interior of such a reservoir will be lined with asphalt or some other impermeable material.

The bottom of the reservoir may be constructed with inverted arches, to distribute the pressure of the columns if desirable, but this is rarely done.

The conduits to and from the reservoirs are taken usually through the dam, and provided with sluice gates or penstocks at one or both ends.

These penstocks each consist of a heavy metal frame fixed in the conduit, between grooves in which slides a stiffened metal plate. This is raised or lowered by a leading screw running in a fixed block on the back, the screw being turned by hand or machine gearing from a penstock-house above (on the dam).

Some penstocks are raised by chains, but the screw gearing is more satisfactory, and allows of a fine adjustment.

In the case of sloping dams, a bridge is usually constructed from the top of the dam to the head of a shaft over the inside entrance to the conduit, so as to give access in the event of stoppage. Similar penstocks are used throughout sewer systems.

Sufficient has been said to show the great importance of hydraulic engineering. Water is now used for all varieties of pressing and lifting machinery, for transmitting sewage and drinking water, and for operating various machines. It is not too much to say that in the near future its use will be extended to almost all varieties of work. For small distances and low velocities it is more economical than electric power, and in many cases much more convenient. It is not so useful when there is a greatly varying load, but wherever the work to be done is reasonably constant, it is, if anything, preferable to electricity.

It has the great advantage over all other sources of power that no conversion is required in the nature of energy. Water situated anywhere and possessing energy can be utilised for power purposes simply by taking off conduits of sufficient capacity and inclinaton, and from them work is drawn.

Contrasting this with heat engines, with or without electricity generation, we have the conversion of the naturally-stored chemical energy into heat by reason of the affinity of the substances (coal or oil) for the atmospheric oxygen, and the conversion of this heat (molecular motion) into motion of the machinery by the expansion of the gas. The loss of energy in this method is enormously greater than that in the hydraulic mains in most cases. With electric conversion, there is further loss in the transmission machinery, and the magnetic leakage and resistance of the dynamo. On the other hand, the great advantage of electric or heat engines,

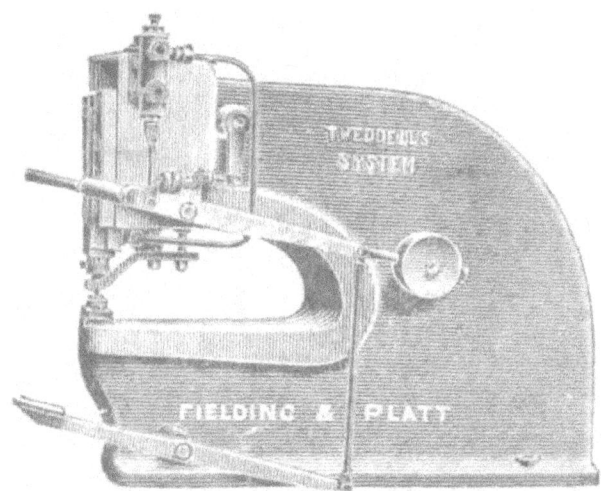

Fig. 23.—Punching Machine.

where high velocities are needed, is indisputable. High velocities with water are quite prohibited on account of the great pressures produced on stoppage. Owing to the incompressibility of water there is no cushioning effect, such as we get in heat engines.

Water pressure is also peculiarly suitable for testing purposes, as enormous forces can be exerted. and yet, when fracture occurs, this immediately ceases, simply being converted into energy of motion. No explosion, such as would occur with steam or pneumatic pressure, appears with water.

The majority of testing machines for both direct tension and compression, internal and external surface pressure, and bending are operated by hydraulic presses, and in this direction there will probably be further development.

INDEX.

JOHN HEYWOOD LTD., Excelsior Printing and Bookbinding Works, Manchester.

www.ingramcontent.com/pod-product-compliance
Lightning Source LLC
Chambersburg PA
CBHW081226280526
45787CB00006B/2535